The Holistic Curriculum

The Holistic Curriculum

John P. Miller

Research in Education / 17

OISE Press

The Ontario Institute for Studies in Education

Education has three prime functions: to conduct ation, to undertake research in education, and e findings of educational studies. The Institute he Ontario Legislature in 1965. It is affiliated with the University of Toronto for graduate studies purposes.

The publications program of the Institute has been established to make available information and materials arising from studies in education, to foster the spirit of critical inquiry, and to provide a forum for the exchange of ideas about education. The opinions expressed should be viewed as those of the contributors.

© The Ontario Institute for Studies in Education 1993
252 Bloor Street West
Toronto, Ontario
M5S 1V6

Canadian Cataloguing in Publication Data

Miller, John P., 1943-
  The holistic curriculum

(Research in education series ; 17)
Bibliography: p.
ISBN 0-7744-0320-9

1. Education — Philosophy. 2. Education — Curricula.
3. Curriculum planning. I. Title. II. Series.

LB1025.2.M44 1988   370'.1   C88-093659-2

ISBN 0-7744-0320-9   Printed in Canada
        4   5   6   7   UTP   69   59   49   39

Contents

Acknowledgments

While *The Holistic Curriculum* is about connectedness, the book, too, has its own set of connections. It arose specifically from a course I teach with the same title. The students with whom I have worked have helped me develop so many of the ideas that I present here. They have also provided the main inspiration for this book.

I would like to thank Al Aschuler and John Eisenberg for their comments on the first draft. Al Alschuler provided many suggestions which were very helpful in making revisions; John Eisenberg has provided invaluable support to me in my work and at the same time never fails to challenge me as he challenges so many of my other colleagues.

John McConnell at OISE Press, who has done the editing, is also to be thanked for his careful and thorough work on the text. I would also like to thank Hugh Oliver, Editor-in-Chief, for his critical support of this work.

Joan Graziani typed the manuscript with care, and I thank her for the long hours she spent with this book.

OISE is also to be thanked for providing a study leave in 1987 so that I could write this book.

Finally, I thank my wife, Jean, and my children, Patrick and Nancy, who had to tolerate my work, which included a computer and printer on the dining table during much of my leave.

Material used in chapter 1 first appeared in the *Journal of Curriculum and Supervision* and is reprinted with permission;

p. 22. Figure from *The Death of the Soul* by William Barrett. © 1986 by William Barrett. Reprinted by permission of Doubleday, a division of Bantam, Doubleday, Dell Publishing Group, Inc.

p. 33. From *Vedanta* by C. Johnson. Copyright © Vedanta Press, Hollywood, Ca.

p. 35. Diagram illustrating Carl Jung's concept of the Self, from *Seeing with the Mind's Eye* by Mike Samuels, M.D., and Nancy Samuels, illustrated by Susan Ida Smith. Copyright © Random House, Inc.

p. 36. Figure 1: "Our Psyche" from *What We May Be* by Piero Ferrucci. Copyright

Introduction

Why the Holistic Curriculum?

The problems of our age are almost innumerable, but it is safe to say environmental destruction and the threat of nuclear war would be at the top of anyone's list.

Our environmental difficulties continue to mount. Acid rain, global deforestation, the massive dumping of chemicals into lakes and rivers, and the deterioration of the ozone layer are just a few of the problems that continue to plague us (Woodwell et al, 1983). Although sensitivity to environmental issues has increased in the last two decades and some gains have been made, these seem minute compared to the environmental problems that still confront us.

Despite the superpower agreement of December 1987 to destroy medium-range nuclear missiles, the threat of nuclear war continues to hover over our heads. Every two months the United States continues to build two hundred nuclear warheads. Two decades ago, Robert McNamara suggested that two hundred nuclear warheads were enough to cripple the Soviet Union. However, the U.S. and Russia continue to be locked in the arms race and today there exist approximately fifty thousand nuclear weapons in the world (Sivard, 1983). We continue to speculate about the effects of nuclear war and "nuclear winters," but we really don't grasp the total horror of its prospect. To be sure, civilization and even life as we know it would disappear.

How can we begin to deal with these problems which are so overwhelming? I believe that one of the principal causes of our difficulties is the fragmentation of life. The industrialist ignores the pollution from his plant because he limits his focus to short-term profits. In our world we compartmentalize to the extent that we no longer see relationships; thus, we have our "private" and "public" lives. Ibsen, in his play *The Doll's House*, describes a businessman who draws strong boundaries between his business and his family life. He describes how this artificial separation leads to the businessman's downfall.

In academia, Kaplan (1961) has referred to the way the analytic philosopher separates his or her work from more fundamental concerns. Value commitments "belong to the personal life of the philosopher but are not integrated with his professional concerns. What he identifies as philosophy is not something that he lives by, but a purely intellectual pursuit, like the study of mathematics or physics with which it is so intimately associated" (p. 88). Just as the industrialist does not see the relationship between his business and the destruction of the environment, the analytic philosopher dismisses the connection between her work and her deepest personal values.

One of the most prevalent forms of the fragmentation of life is our division of people into "us" and "them." At this level we ignore our basic connectedness as human beings. Here we can divide people according to color, people that believe in a particular "ism" from those that don't, and ultimately people that must be bombed in order to preserve our "way of life." It is much easier to build the bomb when you view the enemy as "them." It becomes much more difficult when we see the enemy as "us."

In general, we have atomized our universe so that we can control it. Yet today we are reeling under the effects of the atomization. At the core of this separation is the division we have made between our inner and outer worlds — or between consciousness and the cosmos. Kant said: "Two things fill the mind with ever new and increasing admiration and awe, the oftener and more steadily we reflect upon them: the starry heavens above and the moral law within me." Kant's connection between our inner being and the universe is precisely what we appear to have lost. Buddhism refers to this connection as the principle of *ichinene sanzen* (Ikeda, 1985). Our dualistic approach in the West has lead to the separation, even alienation, between our psyche and the material world. Griffiths (1982) summarizes this split very well:

> It is a disease of the merely rational mind that causes us to see them as separate from one another, to imagine a world extended outside us in space and time, and the mind as something separate from the external world. In reality the world we see is a world which has been penetrated by our consciousness; it is the world as mirrored in the human mind. (p. 58)

It can be argued that schooling contributes to atomization and alienation. We divide our curriculum into subjects, then the subjects into units which, in many cases, are not related to each other. The most extreme example of this segmentation is competency-based education. Tanner and Tanner (1980) comment on the effects of the atomization of the curriculum:

> But perhaps the most damaging result of breaking down the curriculum into minute particles is that it must, of necessity, lead away from an understanding of the unity of knowledge. Obviously, also, a disintegrated curriculum is not likely to help the student develop an integrated outlook or philosophy or lead to transfer of learning. (p. 337)

Another damaging segmentation in education is the way we separate the head and the heart. We stress the basics or thinking skills, but caring and compassion are rarely addressed. Gandhi (1980) realized the futility of this split:

> I hold that true education of the intellect can only come through a proper exercise and training of the bodily organs, e.g., hands, feet, eyes, ears, nose, etc. In other words an intelligent use of the bodily organs in a child provides the best and quickest way of developing his intellect. But unless the development of the mind and body goes hand in hand with a corresponding awakening of the soul, the former alone would prove to be a poor lopsided affair. By spiritual training I mean education of the heart. A proper and allround development of the mind, therefore, can take place only when it proceeds *pari passu* with the education of the physical and spiritual faculties of the child. They constitute an indivisible whole. According to this theory, therefore, it would be a gross fallacy to suppose that they can be developed piecemeal or independently of one another. (p. 138)

2

We continue to ignore Gandhi's insight. Commissions focus primarily on student achievement, parent groups cry out for the basics, and academics argue for thinking skills. Yet the teacher must face a whole child who can never be limited by our categories or priorities. Ultimately, we must engage the child in all her richness rather than reduce her to our own preconceptions.

Education, then, has played its role in contributing to the fragmentation of modern life. In this book I attempt to discuss an alternative approach to education. For want of a better word this approach is called *holistic*. What do I mean by holistic education? Various philosophers and educators have offered definitions which could be interpreted as holistic. For example, Friedrich Froebel (1887), known for the development of kindergarten, said:

> By education, then, the divine essence of man should be unfolded, brought out, lifted into consciousness, and man himself raised into free, conscious obedience to the divine principle that lives in him, and to a free representation of this principle in his life.
>
> Education in instruction would lead man to see and know the divine, spiritual, and eternal principle which animates surrounding nature, constitutes the essence of nature, and is permanently manifested in nature. (pp. 4-5)

Krishnamurti (1974), the Indian spiritual teacher who died in 1986, stated:

> The function of your teachers is to educate not only the partial mind but the totality of the mind; to educate you so that you do not get caught in the little whirlpool of existence but live in the whole river of life. This is the whole function of education. The right kind of education cultivates your whole being, the totality of your mind. It gives your mind and heart a depth, an understanding of beauty. (p. 46)

Finally, Rudolph Steiner (1986), the founder of Waldorf education said:

> For it is essential that we should develop an art of education which will lead us out of the social chaos into which we have fallen during the last few years and decades. And the only way out of this social chaos is to bring spirituality into the souls of men through education, so that out of the spirit itself men may find the way to progress and the further evolution of civilization.
>
> We know in our hearts that this is true, for the world is created in spirit and comes forth out of spirit, and so also human creation can only be fruitful if it springs forth from the fountain head of spirit itself. But to achieve such fruitful creation out of spirit, man must be educated and taught in the spirit also. (p. 314)

I offer the following definition:

> The focus of holistic education is on relationships — the relationship between linear thinking and intuition, the relationship between mind and body, the relationships between various domains of knowledge, the relationship between the individual and community, and the relationship between self and Self. In the holistic curriculum the student examines these relationships so that he/she gains both an awareness of them and the skills necessary to transform the relationships where it is appropriate.

This definition centres on connection and this definition will be explored in a number of different contexts in this book. Another way of clarifying holistic education is to compare it to other forms of education.

In several contexts (Miller, 1983; Miller and Seller, 1985; Miller, 1986; and Miller, 1987) I have described three basic positions that are helpful in analysing and describing curriculum and instruction. What do I mean by a curriculum position? A curriculum position is rooted in a worldview that can be linked to various philosophical, psychological, and social contexts. Let me briefly describe the three positions — transmission, transaction, and transformation. The last of these positions — the transformation — is holistic.

Transmission

The *transmission position* focusses on traditional school subjects taught through traditional teaching methods. In this position there is primarily a one-way movement wherein the student imbibes certain values, skills, and knowledge. The position is outlined in the following diagram:

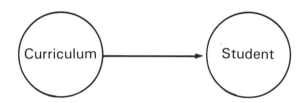

Transmission Position

There are two strands within the transmission position. One strand focusses on a traditional academic approach. William T. Harris (1880), the nineteenth-century American educator, represented this approach when he argued that the textbook should be at the centre of learning because it reflects "what has been tested and found essential to civilization" (p. 9). Today, Neil Postman (1979) has picked up this argument in his conviction that schools should focus on teaching "systematic content" (p. 214). For Postman the curriculum is "but a design for controlling and shaping the minds of the young" (p. 88).

The other strand within the transmission position concentrates on a mechanistic view of learning. The stimulus-response (S-R) model of the behaviorists represents this approach. The student is viewed passively as someone who responds to the initiatives of the teacher, the computer, or the programmed text. The American psychologist E. L. Thorndike (1916) can be seen as representative of the transmission position when he states that "teaching is the arrangement of situations which will lead to desirable bonds" (p. 174).

Underlying both strands, however, is an atomistic worldview that sees nature as composed of isolated building blocks. This worldview not only underlies the transmission curriculum that is segmented into subjects and programmed units, but also the philosophical, psychological, and economic contexts that surround the curriculum.

For example, the transmission curriculum (as in back to the basics) can often be popular in a conservative (laissez-faire) economic climate. In laissez-faire theory the individual is atomized in the market place as he or she competes with other individuals. Psychologically, I have already referred to behavioral psychology that tends to break human behavior into isolated components so that it can be controlled through reinforcement programs. Finally, the transmission position can be linked with logical positivism, which is concerned with breaking down language into logical components that can be analysed and verified. In the early twentieth century, Bertrand Russell was part of a philosophical school called *logical atomism* that is particularly representative of an atomistic approach to philosophy.

Transaction

In the *transaction position,* the individual is seen as rational and capable of intelligent problem-solving. Education is viewed as a dialogue between the student and the curriculum in which the student reconstructs knowledge through the dialogue process. The following diagram outlines this position.

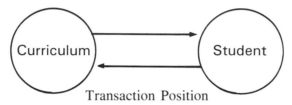

Transaction Position

The transaction position focusses on problem-solving and instructional strategies that facilitate problem-solving. These strategies can sometimes lie within specific academic disciplines, or they can be interdisciplinary. They can also be applied to social problems that occur within a democratic context.

The worldview or paradigm underlying the transaction position is the scientific method. This view is at the heart of John Dewey's pragmatism, which focussed on the application of the scientific method to a broad range of problems. Dewey (1938/1969) argued that the scientific method is "the only authentic means at our command for getting at the significance of our everyday experiences of the world in which we live" (p. 88). In the transmission position science is viewed mechanistically; in the transaction position science and the scientific method are seen as vehicles which can help the individual constructively deal with the world.

In psychology, Lawrence Kohlberg (1972) has argued that the developmental theories of Piaget and himself represent an attempt to clarify Dewey's work in psychological terms. Piaget's work advances the view that development results from interaction between the student and a stimulating intellectual environment. Kohlberg argues that cognitive developmental theory is an extension of Dewey's conception of growth. The political ideology linked with the transaction position is small "l" liberalism, in which there is general belief that rational intelligence can improve the social environment. Transaction economists, such as John Kenneth Galbraith, believe that the economy can be improved through rational planning and government intervention. This political orientation is characterized by human rights legislation to ensure that minority ethnic groups have equal opportunity to participate in society.

Transformation

The *transformation position* concentrates on personal and social change. In this position there is a holistic emphasis, and the student is not just viewed in the cognitive mode, but in terms of his or her aesthetic, moral, physical, and spiritual needs. Thus, the curriculum and the child do not just interact at a cognitive level (the transaction position), but interconnect in a holistic manner. This interconnection is diagrammed below.

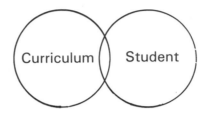

Transformation Position

There are two strands within the transformation position. One strand, the humanistic, is rooted in a concern for individual growth; the other strand centres on social change. In the humanistic strand, educators such as Froebel, Tolstoy, A. S. Neill, and John Holt have viewed the child as essentially good and have argued that the role of the teacher is to let this positive potential unfold. A. S. Neill expressed this belief in his book *Summerhill* when he says:

> When my first wife and I began the school, we had one main idea: to make the school fit the child — instead of making the child fit the school . . .
>
> Well, we set out to make a school in which we should allow children freedom to be themselves. In order to do this, we had to renounce all discipline, all direction, all suggestion, all moral training, all religious instruction. We have been called brave, but it did not require courage. All it required was what we had — a complete belief in the child as a good, not an evil, being. For almost forty years, this belief in the goodness of the child has never wavered; it rather has become a final faith. (p. 4)

The other strand, that of social change, is seen, in part, in the work of such theorists as Michael Apple and Henry Giroux. These educators argue that schooling reflects social, economic, and political structures so that schools in capitalist societies help reproduce the capitalist system. They advocate political and social change that will create a more egalitarian and co-operative society.

The two strands in the transformation positions have sometimes conflicted with each other. For example, staff in alternative schools often have battled over whether schools should facilitate individual growth or, instead, be more politically motivated. The position is most effective when the two strands are integrated. Florence Tager (1986) describes an examples of this in the Modern School of New York and Stelton.

What is the relationship between the three positions? One way is to see them as competing alternatives wherein one must choose one position to the exclusion of the others. Another alternative is to see each position as being more inclusive. From this framework the transaction position would include the transmission position focus

6

on knowledge retention and would apply it to problem-solving. In turn, the transformation position with its holistic emphasis would incorporate the cognitive thrust of the transaction position within a broader, more inclusive context. It is thus possible to view the three positions as concentric circles:

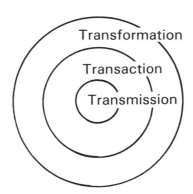

In holistic education, then, we attempt to facilitate a broadening of vision and perspective. We move from the more restrictive scope of an atomistic perspective to a more inclusive view that witnesses the connections between ourselves and the universe.

If we are to confront the fragmentation and the problems associated with fragmentation, such as pollution and nuclear war, then the transformation position, or holistic education, demands our attention. Certainly, holistic education will not solve the problems of our age, but along with other personal and societal changes we can begin to confront our alienation.

Some of these societal changes are discussed in chapter 3. In the first part of this book the context and background of the holistic curriculum are examined. In chapter 1 the philosophical context of holism — the perennial philosophy — is discussed in relation to atomism and pragmatism. In the second chapter the psychological context is examined.

In the second half of the book I discuss the holistic curriculum and how it can facilitate various pedagogical connections; for example, the connection between linear thinking and intuition (chapter 5), body–mind connections (chapter 6), subject connections (chapter 7), connections with community (chapter 8), and Self connections (chapter 9).

References

Dewey, J. *Experience and Education.* New York: Macmillan/Collier Books, 1969. (Originally published in 1938.)

Froebel, R. *The Education of Man.* New York: Herder and Herder, 1887.

Gandhi, M. *All Men Are Brothers: Autobiographical Reflections.* Edited by Krishna Kripalani. New York: Continuum. 1980.

Harris, W. T. "Textbooks and Their Uses." *Education* 1(9) (1880).

Ikeda, Daisku. *Buddhism and the Cosmos*. London: Macdonald, 1985.

Kaplan, A. *The New World of Philosophy*. New York: Random House, 1961.

Krishnamurti, J. *On Education*. New York: Harper and Row, 1974.

Kohlberg, L., and Mayer, R. "Development as an Aim of Education," *The Harvard Educational Review* 42 (1972), 449-96.

Miller, J. *The Educational Spectrum*. New York: Longman, 1983.

Miller, J. "Atomism, Pragmatism, and Holism." *Journal of Curriculum and Supervision* 1 (1986), 175-96.

Miller, J. "Transformation as Aim of Education." *Journal of Curriculum Theorizing* 7:1 (1987), 94-152.

Miller, J., and Seller, W. *Curriculum: Perspectives and Practice*. New York: Longman, 1985.

Neil, A. S. *Summerhill: A Radical Approach to Child Rearing*. New York: Hart Publishing Co., 1960.

Postman, N. *Teaching as a Conserving Activity*. New York: Dell Books, 1979.

Steiner, R. "The Roots of Education." In *The Essential Steiner,* edited by R. A. McDermott. New York: Harper and Row, 1968.

Sivard, R. *World Military and Social Expenditures*. Lessburg, Va.: World Priorities, 1979, 1981, 1983.

Tager, F. "The Modern School of New York and Stelton." *Curriculum Inquiry* 16 (1986), 391-416.

Tanner, D., and Tanner, L. *Curriculum Development: Theory into Practice*. New York: MacMillan, 1980.

Thorndike, E. *Educational Psychology: Briefer Course*. New York: Teacher's College Press, 1916.

Woodwell, G., et al. "Global Deforestation: Contribution to Atmospheric Carbon Dioxide." *Science* 222 (1983), 1081-1086.

Part I

Holistic Curriculum:
The Context

1

The Philosophic Context: The Perennial Philosophy

The perennial philosophy (Huxley, 1970) provides the philosophic underpinnings of the holistic curriculum. The perennial philosophy holds that all life is connected in an interdependent universe. Stated differently, we experience relatedness through a fundamental ground of being. Before examining the perennial philosophy, I would like to review the philosophic contexts of the transmission and transaction positions — atomism and pragmatism. This review, I believe, provides an argument for holism as the most adequate philosophic context for curriculum.

Atomism

The atomistic view of reality can be traced to Greece where Democritus conceived of Nature as empty space and atoms. He saw atoms as small, indivisible units piled upon one another; the indivisible atom, then, lay at the core of all substance. Democritus was a deterministic atomist who saw the motion of atoms not as random events but as the consequence of specific causes which would have yielded no other event.

Today, the Greek view has been replaced by a more sophisticated atomism. Contemporary atomism can be characterized by the following principles:

1. Reality is seen through materialism.
2. This reality can be reduced to logical components or atoms.
3. We know through our senses.
4. We can use the findings of empiricism to develop a technology to control the material world.
5. It is possible to approach inquiry from a value neutral perspective.

Reality Is Seen through Materialism

Thomas Hobbes, the seventeenth-century philosopher, was a materialist and argued that nature consisted of an aggregate of things outside our mind. Hobbes focussed, then, on natural philosophy, which is concerned with the properties of bodies. Today, materialism has been modified into various forms of positivism where science is seen as the basis for understanding matter and for discovering the laws that regulate the interaction of bodies. Contemporary materialism has been called physicalism or the idea that all sciences can be reformulated in the language of physics. According to Ayer (1984), physicalism "is held by those who believe that the physical world is a closed system; that everything that happens can be accounted for in physical terms." (p. 13)

Reality Can Be Reduced to Logical Components or Atoms

In philosophy, Logical Atomism expressed this principle and Barrett (1978) has summarized this view:

> Logic analyzes statements into two kinds: complex or molecular statements, on the one hand, and, on the other, the atomic statements into which these are resolved . . . The world must ultimately be made up of atomic facts that correspond to the atomic statements with which logical analysis terminates. And the various groupings of these atomic facts make up the complex facts that constitute our experience. We thus arrive at the full-fledged doctrine of Logical Atomism. (p. 39)

Wittgenstein took Logical Atomism to its most radical conclusion when he said "any one can either be the case or not be the case, and everything else remains the same." In Wittgenstein's universe the atoms, or facts, are not connected. Leibniz also atomized the universe into his monads. These monads, however, are linked through Leibniz's conception of God, the ultimate Monad. In Wittgenstein's world his "facts" do not enjoy a unity of any kind.

We Know through Our Senses

Empiricism, which regards observations by the senses as the only reliable source of knowledge, has been developed most fully in the English philosophical tradition — in the seventeenth and eighteenth centuries by John Locke and David Hume, and in this century in analytic philosophy.

Hume was the most radical of the enlightenment empiricists and his work is still a reference point for empirical thinking. Hume argued that the contents of consciousness are perceptions, and he divides perceptions into impressions and ideas. Impressions are our immediate sensations and emotions while ideas are copies or images of impressions. Hume claims that all ideas are derived from impressions; if one cannot link an idea with an original impression then the idea is meaningless. According to Lavine (1984), "Hume has presented a view of our experience as made up of atomic elements, of distinct and separable impressions and ideas, each an atom constituting our experience" (p. 155). Hume's empiricism is similar to Wittgenstein's atomism in that there is no link or causal connection between the impressions. Lavine (1984) claims:

> But not only are metaphysics and science impossible, so too is the common sense knowledge of everyday life, with its accounts of the necessary causal connections between fire and the burning of a finger held to it, between smoking cigarettes and lung cancer, betwen the planting of seeds and the growth of plants. These necessary connections of common sense are reduced to psychological associa-

tions of ideas; there is no justification for their providing explanations or predictions of events. (p. 168).

Just as logical atomism and analytic philosophy makes us skeptical of our common sense knowledge so Hume's empiricism makes us skeptical of causality in everyday life. Hume's empiricism and Wittgenstein's analytical philosophy leave us in a disconnected universe of atoms. Barrett (1978) states:

> But this ordinary practical freedom of ours becomes a theoretical impossibility in the fragmented world of Hume and Wittgenstein. In that world there is no continuity of becoming at all — no causal influx of the present into the future. One atomic fact follows another without connection. I reach out to grasp my pen in order to put these words down, and what I thus perform as the simple and continuous act of my will is now supposed, in the Humean view, to fall apart into disjointed fragments. (pp. 50-51)

Positivists such as Auguste Comte and Rudolph Carnap rejected the random atomism of Hume, instead, they developed a deterministic atomism. In general, there is a tension in the atomistic worldview between randomness and determinism. Some theorists shudder at Hume's world and instead build a world of absolute determinism. For these positivists causality is not a connection of sense impressions, but rooted in the physical world and discoverable through scientific investigation. For Comte, empirical science is the only reliable source of knowledge and thus should remove all ideas that cannot be verified through scientific investigation. Scientific knowledge should also be extended to make technology "no longer excessively geometrical, mechanical, or chemical, but also primarily political and moral." (Quoted in Schon, 1983, p. 32)

Logical positivism consists of two distinct worlds. On the one hand, there is the world of everyday existence; on the other, there is the world of scientific verification. In this latter world we supposedly have access to "truth" or at least "objective reality." The former world is suspect as we learn not to trust our everyday sense of how things are but instead accord scientific verification a higher status as a source of understanding and relating to the world. In this view we are encouraged to deny our intuitive insight into how things are in favor of a more abstract view validated by mechanistic science.

Empiricism Can Be Used to Develop a Technology to Control Our Behavior and the Environment

Skinner's behavioral psychology extends the Comtean notion of technological control to human behavior. In 1984 he published *The Technology of Teaching*, in which he asserts that "recent improvements in the conditions which control behavior in the field of learning are of two principal sorts" (1984, p. 10), both of which result from recognition and applications of the law of effect: first, we can use this law to shape "the behavior of an organism almost at will" (1984, p. 10); and, second, we can use it to "maintain behavior in given states of strength for long periods of time" (1984, p. 10). Skinner is referring here to the use of reinforcers, which is the central component in his theory of operant conditioning. Education, in Skinner's view, is a matter of choosing and using reinforcement techniques; teaching is "the arrangement of contingencies of reinforcement under which students learn" (1984, p. 64). By arranging reinforcers in specific ways, the teacher can increase certain desired behaviors. It is clear that Skinner's psychology is atomistic: his programmed learning techniques break down behavior into small bits that can be manipulated; small identifiable components are used to organize student progress by means of sequential steps.

It Is Possible to Approach Inquiry from a Value Neutral Perspective

In an atomistic universe where all elements are more or less equal, values are not a central consideration. In pursuing inquiry, the central concerns of the empiricist are not ethical in nature, but concentrate rather on generating new knowledge that can be validated by science. Thus, positivists and empiricists have not generally been concerned with values questions. In education, competency-based education and mastery learning are rarely concerned with ethics; instead, the focus is on mastery of specific competencies. We turn now to how the atomistic and empirical traditions are manifested in educational practice.

Atomism and the Curriculum

Atomism in the curriculum has stressed segmentation and reduction of the curriculum into small, separate units. An individual who articulated an atomistic perspective in the first part of this century was Franklin Bobbitt. Bobbitt (1924) wrote, "let us discover what the activities are which make up man's life and we have the objectives of education" (p. 24). The objectives of Bobbitt's curriculum correspond to the daily activities of adults. Since these activities are almost infinite in number, the objectives and the curriculum are reduced to twenty or thirty thousand specific mechanical skills or behaviors. Clearly this is curriculum that is atomistic at its core. Except for some broad categories, there is no attempt to conceptualize or draw a link among these large number of objectives. Bobbitt's (1924) categories include:

1. Language activities; social intercommunication.
2. Health activities.
3. Citizenship activities.
4. General social activities — meeting and mingling with others.
5. Space-time activities, amusements, recreations.
6. Keeping one's self mentally fit — analogous to the health activities of keeping fit.
7. Religious activities.
8. Parental activities, the upbringing of children, the maintenance of a proper home life.
   (pp. 7-8)

Snedden was a sociologist who supported the views of Bobbitt. He divided the large number of objectives into production and consumption categories. According to Tanner and Tanner (1980), this led to further compartmentalization of vocation and culture, as the effect of the Bobbitt–Snedden approach was to "atomize subject matter in the mind of both teacher and learner." (p. 336). The Bobbitt–Snedden view is based on a mechanistic view of science, as the universe is reducible to separate, isolated components. Atomistic approaches to education are still with us today. Clearly competency-based education and related approaches such as mastery learning reflect an atomistic conception of the curriculum. Competency-based education involves: (1) the selection of competency statements; (2) the specification of evaluation indicators to assess competency achievements; and (3) the development of an appropriate instructional system.

According to McAshan (1979), competency-based education is based on behavioral learning theory.

> Learning theory indicates that learning begins when stimuli (either internal or external) and their reinforcement cause an organism to react. Learning occurs through this process, and the more complex cognitive, psychomotor, and affective motivational systems develop. Thus, all learning can be said to begin when the learner is sensitized to the existence of stimuli. These stimuli may be thought of as occurring from the result of teaching strategies (or enabling activities that are part of the instructional delivery system in CBE programs. (p. 51)

Behaviorism, then, provides the psychological context for atomistic approaches to curriculum and instruction.

Today mastery learning can also be seen as an example of the atomistic paradigm. Joyce and Weil (1980) define a central component of mastery learning as "the curriculum . . . divided into a larger set of relatively small learning units, each one accompanied by its own objectives" (p. 447). In mastery learning it is essential that the curriculum be reduced to small units so the student can proceed in a sequential way. Thus the student masters each unit or segment until a designated level of mastery is achieved.

Pragmatism

John Dewey was critical of atomistic perspective and he and other pragmatists such as William James rejected a philosophy which segmented experience. In contrast, pragmatism embraces the following principles:

1. The universe is in process, all things are changing.
2. Experimental science is the best model for interpreting and acting upon experience.
3. Hypotheses tested by experience, then, constitute the best form of knowledge.
4. The scientific method can also be applied to social problems and social experience.
5. Values arise from particular contexts and consequences.

The Universe Is in Process — All Things Are Changing

John Childs, a colleague of Dewey, stated that "the world is characterized by process and change." The world, to the pragmatist, is like an ongoing stream where everything is in a state of flux. Related to this notion is the idea that the world is incomplete and indeterminate. In the positivist view the universe tends to be seen as a closed system which functions as a machine. The pragmatists, however, do not accept this view; instead they see a more open universe that is in flux and indeterminate. William James spoke of an open universe with its lid off.

Experimental Science Is the Best Model for Interpreting Experience

Dewey (1938/1963) argued that the scientific method is the best model of intelligent behavior:

> It means that scientific method is the only authentic means at our command for getting at the significance of our everyday experiences of the world in which we live. It means that scientific method provides a working pattern of the way in which and the conditions under which experiences are used to lead ever onward and outward. Adaptation of the method to individuals of various degrees of maturity is a problem for the educator, and the constant factors in the problem are the formation of ideas, acting upon ideas, observation of the conditions which result, and organization of facts and ideas for future use. (p. 88)

Dewey (1916/1966) developed a problem-solving method for analysing experience based on the scientific method. The method consists of five steps:

(1)   perplexity, confusion, doubt due to the fact that one is implicated in an incomplete situation whose full character is not yet determined;

(ii)   a conjectural anticipation — a tentative interpretation of the given elements, attributing to them a tendency to effect certain consequences;

(iii)   a careful survey (examination, inspection, exploration, analysis) of all attainable consideration which will define and clarify the problem at hand;

(iv)   a consequent elaboration of the tentative hypothesis to make it more precise and more consistent, because squaring with a wider range of fact;

(v)   taking one stand upon the projected hypothesis as a plan of action which is applied to the existing state of affairs: doing something overtly to bring about the anticipated result, and thereby testing the hypothesis. (pp. 150-151)

The first step indicates that the individual is confronted with a problem or an ''indeterminate situation.'' Dewey (1938) characterizes the indeterminate situation as ''disturbed, troubled, ambiguous, confused, full of conflicting tendencies'' (p. 105).

In the next step the person examines the elements and their possible consequences associated with these elements in this particular situation.

In the third step the individual attempts to clear up any confusion encountered by defining the problem. The person, then, formulates the problem so that it can be solved without excessive trial and error and busy work.

In the fourth step the person begins to try out in his/her mind possible solutions to the problem. A tentative hypothesis, then, is developed.

In the final step the hypothesis is tested against experience. If the problem is not solved, then a new hypothesis is developed.

Dewey's problem-solving sequence applies the scientific method to reflective experience. Pragmatism overcomes the division that atomism developed between science

15

and everyday experience. Science is not elevated above everyday experience but instead is applied to pluralistic contexts.

Hypotheses Tested by Experience Constitute the Best Form of Knowledge

Pragmatism, in general, and John Dewey, specifically, reject the atomistic concern for the collection and categorization of factual knowledge. Although the content of the observation is important to the pragmatist, the method of observation and reflection as outlined above is even more critical. Reflective experience, then, becomes the organizer of facts.

Dewey and the pragmatists were also critical of the passive view of the mind which is associated with empiricism. Locke and other empiricists viewed the mind as a blank slate which receives data in the form of sense impressions. In pragmatism knowlege is viewed in a more active mode. Sense impressions are gathered, but they are used to develop hypotheses which are then tested against experience. The mind, then, is not just passively receiving data but is generating meaning through experience. The person engages the world through experience and this engagement allows the person to test out hypotheses and ideas in an active manner.

Butler (1950) makes the following claim about the epistemology of pragmatism:

> It can be seen that the precise word for describing knowledge for pragmatism is not the adjective, *experiential*, which might be acceptable to many idealists, but rather the descriptive, *experimental*. Because what is known is always known on the way to achieving a satisfactory outworking of a given unit of experience. What is known is a hypothesis working satisfactorily; the resolving course of action in an experiment, not just an item of knowlege but an item of value in addition being made actual in experience. (p. 449)

The Scientific Method in the Form of Reflective Intelligence Should Be Applied to Social Experience

Dewey was a strong advocate of a democracy which allows for the growth of each person and the exercise of intelligence. The development of intelligence, in Dewey's view, is fundamental to democracy and is the main goal of education. The school's main function, then, is the fostering of reflective intelligence as students should learn to reflect on social experience and to test out hypotheses in terms of this experience.

Kaplan (1961) has linked pragmatism and liberalism when he says that the method of pragmatic liberalism is "the application of intelligence to social problems." The basic assumption of pragmatism is that reflective intelligence and the scientific method can resolve most problems.

Values from a Pragmatic Perspective Arise from Particular Contexts and Consequences

In pragmatism a value judgment assesses whether a certain action will have certain consequences of experienced satisfaction or frustration. It declares whether something will help attain a specific goal or end. Value judgments must also assess whether the context is appropriate for the desired end. In pragmatism, means and ends/contexts and consequences are viewed in relation to each other. Pragmatism, then, is relativistic. However, pragmatists reject a total relativism in favor of an objective relativism. The reflective method helps the individual avoid making moral choices solely on the basis of whim. Again the scientific method in the form of reflective experience is the critical reference point for the pragmatic perspective.

Pragmatism and the Curriculum

Pragmatism with its emphasis on reflective intelligence has formed the theoretical bases for many inquiry approaches to curriculum. These approaches can be viewed as variations on Dewey's five-step method. For example, Massialas (1975, p. 31) has developed a six-step sequence in social studies:

1. Defining and categorizing concepts and distinguishing between ideas.
2. Clarifying values underlying positions.
3. Collecting and analysing evidence.
4. Using evidence to validate or evaluate hypotheses or positions.
5. Exploring logical consequences of positions.
6. Generalizing.

Herbert Thelen also developed what he called a group investigation approach which reflects a Deweyean conception of inquiry. In this model (Joyce and Weil, 1980) there are six steps:

1. Encounter puzzling situation.
2. Explore reactions to the situation.
3. Formulate main task and organize to study the task.
4. Independent and group study.
5. Analyse progress and process.
6. Begin a new cycle with a problem arising from the investigation.

Although the methods of inquiry vary from project to project, most follow the model of the pragmatic inquiry developed by Dewey.

Holism

Holism is based on the "perennial philosophy" which holds that all things are part of an indivisible unity or whole. In brief, the basic principles of the perennial philosophy and holism can be identified as follows:

1. There is an interconnectedness of reality and a fundamental unity in the universe.
2. There is an intimate connection between the individual's inner or higher self and this unity.
3. In order to see this unity we need to cultivate intuition through contemplation and meditation.
4. Value is derived from seeing and realizing the interconnectedness of reality.

5. The realization of this unity among human beings leads to social activity designed to counter injustice and human suffering.

These principles have been articulated in different spiritual and intellectual traditions in both the East and the West. In the West the perennial philosophy can be traced to early Greek times. For example, the Greek philosopher Pythagoras made the connection between the inner person and the universe. He designated the word *psyche* to represent this "inner self" which corresponds to the highest principles of the universe. The individual must attend to the psyche to realize this connection. According to Jacob Needleman (1982), Pythagoras felt that "the cosmos, the deep order of nature is knowledgeable through self-knowledge — man is a microcosm" (p. 59). Thus the individual must contemplate or meditate to gain access to this understanding. Pythagoras suggested that certain techniques such as "the use of parable and symbol, of meditation, of the discipline of silence, of the study of music and sacred dance" (p. 45) as well as other methods be used in the search for self-knowledge.

Socrates and Plato could also be viewed as part of this holistic thread in the West. Socrates spoke of an inner "voice", which was his conscience. He said, "the voice I seem to hear murmuring in my ears, like the sound of the flute in the ears of the mystic; that voice, I say is humming in my ears and prevents me from hearing any other." (Cited in Capaldi et al., 1981, p. 54.) This voice which comes from the person's intuitive centre has been a source of individual conscience for centuries. Gandhi and Martin Luther King spoke of the same voice.

Plato thought sense knowledge was the least reliable form of knowing. The highest form of knowledge is a kind of recollection where the person recovers his or her innate thoughts. Sense experience, in fact, can interfere with this recollection which, instead, occurs through philosophic contemplation. (Capaldi et al., 1981, p. 72.)

It is possible to identify the perennial philosophy, or at least aspects of the philosophy, with Eastern spiritual traditions (Hinduism, in the person of Gandhi, for example). Western Idealism (Mary Calkins), Transcendentalism (Emerson), some forms of Existentialism (Heidegger), and Christian Mysticism (Thomas Merton). We turn now to the five principles.

The Interconnected Nature of Reality and the Fundamental Unity of the Universe

In atomism the universe is viewed as a collection of atoms; in pragmatism it is seen as an ongoing process; in holism it is perceived as harmonious and interconnected. Holism acknowledges the individual part and that things are in process; however, there is a fundamental unity underlying the process and connecting the parts. This unity, though, is not monistic; instead, the emphasis is on the *relations* between the whole and the part. According to Mary Whiton Calkins (1930), the American idealist philosopher:

> The ultimately real relations are those of whole and part, of including and being included. The beings of the universe are, from this point of view, all of them parts of some including entity, and are thus related to each other indirectly. (pp. 210-211)

Emerson (1965) repeatedly emphasized the relation between the individual person and the Oversoul or "the great soul."

> I am somehow receptive of the great soul, and thereby I do overlook the sun and the stars and feel them to be the fair accidents and effects which change and pass. More and more the surges of everlasting nature enter into me, and I become public and human in my regards and actions. So come I to live in thoughts and act with energies which are immortal. Thus revering the soul, and learning, as the ancient said, that "its beauty is immense," man will come to see that the world is the perennial miracle which the soul worketh, and be less astonished at particular wonders; he will learn that there is no profane history; that all history is sacred; that the universe is represented in an atom, in a moment of time. He will weave no longer a spotted life of shreds and patches, but he will live with a divine unity. (p. 295)

By seeing this relation between ourselves and "the great soul" we become whole.

For Gandhi (1980), this unity reveals itself in the immediacy of daily life. He also claims that this unity lies behind all religions. He said: "The forms are many, but the informing spirit is one. How can there be room for distinctions of high and low where there is this all-embracing fundamental unity underlying the outward diversity? For that is a fact meeting you at every step in daily life. The final goal of all religions is to realize this essential oneness." (p. 63). Gandhi's position that this unity is evident in everyday life reflects the notion that the realization of the interconnectedness of reality should not be relegated to remote forms of mysticism.

Heidegger refers to this fundamental unity as Being and he attempts to awaken in us our relationship to Being. Heidegger felt that modern philosophy has separated us from primal "ground of Being"; by seeing our relation to Being we can realize a basic unity in our lives. According to Heidegger, an awareness of Being leads to "astonishment" or a sense of awe. This astonishment or sense of awe is integral to Holism and is a spur to scientific work and artistic creation as Einstein suggested.

Einstein (1984) spoke of a cosmic religion which involves an awareness of the harmony of nature.

> The individual feels the sublimity and marvelous order which reveal themselves both in nature and in the world of thought. Individual existence impresses him as a sort of prison and he wants to experience the universe as a single significant whole. (p. 102)

There is disagreement among holistic thinkers as to what extent science can contribute to an understanding of this fundamental unity. Einstein spent his life in search of a unified field theory but never succeeded in his quest. Now some physicists are claiming that a grand unified theory of Nature is close at hand. For example, Davies (1984) claims that for the "first time in the history of science we can form a conception of what a complete scientific theory of the world will look like." (p. 149) This statement is based on the discovery of supergravity or the force that holds the neutron and proton together in the nucleus of the atom. Davies (1984) states:

> Supergravity is the crowning achievement in the long search for unity in physics. Although still in its formative stages, it undoubtedly holds out great hope for solv-

ing three major outstanding problems of theoretical physics, i.e., how to unify all four forces of nature into a single superforce, how to explain the existence of all these fundamental particles — they are needed to maintain supersymmetry — and why gravity is so much weaker than the other forces of nature. (p. 148)

At the centre of the vision of the new physics is the idea that a "noncausal, holistic order" (Davies, 1984, p. 220) exists in the universe. In subatomic physics, we can define the position of a subatomic particle (for example, an electron) only in relation to other particles and in relation to the observer and the method of observation. According to Davies, "There is no hope of building a full understanding of matter from the constituent particles alone. Only the system as a whole gives concrete expression to microscopic reality." (p. 39)

However, some of the individuals who were responsible for the development of modern physics claim that science cannot be expected to reveal the true nature of the fundamental unity of existence. Erwin Schroedinger (1984), who discovered a form of "wave mechanics" that became central to quantam mechanics, stated that "science is reticent too when it is a question of the great Unity - the One of Parmenides — of which we all somehow form part, to which we belong" (p. 82). Werner Heisenberg (1984), who developed the Uncertainty Principle, also claimed that "the language of poetry may be more important than the language of science" in interpreting the "one," or "the unitary principle behind the phenomena." (p. 54)

The Intimate Connection Between the Individual's Inner or Higher Self and This Unity

In his journal Emerson (1909) stated:

> A man finds out that there is somewhat in him that knows more than he does. Then he comes presently to the curious question, Who's who? which of these two is really me? the one that knows more or the one that knows less: the little follow or the big fellow. (Vol. 9, p. 190)

Emerson's little fellow is our personal ego which strives to impose its will on the universe. The big fellow, or our higher self, realizes the futility of such endeavors and merely seeks to be in tune with the Universal Mind. When we are in touch with the "big fellow" we "are not to do, but let do, not to work, but to be worked upon." With the little fellow, we strive and manipulate; with the big fellow, we listen and see and, according to Emerson, are subject to a "vast and sudden enlargement of power." Emerson is referring to the creative power that is similar to Einstein's cosmic religion that inspires the artist and the scientist.

Thomas Merton (1959), the American Trappist monk, spoke of the "inner self," which is similar to Emerson's "big fellow."

> Instead of seeing the external world in its bewildering complexity, separateness, and multiplicity; instead of seeing objects as things to be manipulated for pleasure or profit; instead of placing ourselves over against objects in a posture of desire, defiance, suspicion, greed, or fear, the inner self sees the world from a deeper and more spiritual viewpoint. In the language of Zen, it sees things "without affirmation or denial"; that is to say, from a higher vantage point, which is in-

tuitive and concrete and which has no need to manipulate or distort reality by means of slanted concepts and judgments. It simply ''sees'' what it sees, and does not take refuge behind a screen of conceptual prejudices and verbalistic distortions. (p. 17)

The German philosopher Martin Heidegger had a unique vision of the human being. He did not see the person as a skin encapsulated ego, but as a ''force field,'' or what he called *Dasein.* Dasein, then, is intimately connected with the surrounding environment. Barret (1962) comments:

Heidegger's theory of man (and of Being) might be called the Field Theory of Man (or the Field Theory of Matter), provided we take this purely as an analogy; for Heidegger would hold it a spurious and inauthentic way to philosophize to derive one's philosophic conclusions from the highly abstract theories of physics. But in the way that Einstein took matter to be a field (a magnetic field, say) — in opposition to the Newtonian conception of a body as existing inside its surface boundaries — so Heidegger takes man to be a field or region of Being. (pp. 217-18)

Holism, then, attempts to restore the link between Kant's moral law within and the universe which has been severed by atomism.

Cultivation of Intuition and Insight through Contemplation and Meditation

A consistent thread in the perennial philosophy is that the rational or analytic mind which dwells on discrimination cannot fully grasp the wholeness of existence. Instead, intuition should be cultivated in order to see more clearly the interrelatedness of reality. Emerson (1965) refers to intuition as:

The inquiry leads up to that source, at once the essence of genius, of virtue, and of life, which we call Spontaneity or Instinct. We denote this primary wisdom as Intuition, whilst all later teachings are tuitions. In that deep force, the last fact behind which analysis cannot go, all things find their common origin. For, the sense of being which in calm hours rises, we know not how, in the soul, is not diverse from things, from space, from light, from time, from man, but one of them, and proceeds obviously from the same source whence their life and being also proceed. (p. 267)

Similar to Socrates, Gandhi refers to intuition as that ''still small voice within'' that prods him to social action. ''There are moments in your life when you must act, even though you cannot carry your best friends with you. The 'still small voice' within you must always be the final arbiter when there is conflict of duty.'' (p. 62).

Kant also referred to intuition, although he called it reason. He argued that we know in three different ways: (1) sensibility-sense experience; (2) understanding-conceptual and scientific intelligence; and (3) reason which intuits transcendent ideas. These categories parallel knowledge within the transmission (sensibility), transaction (understanding), and transformation (reason) frameworks. Barrett (1986) has diagrammed that relation between the three Kantian forms of knowledge which is similar to the diagram of the three positions presented in the Introduction.

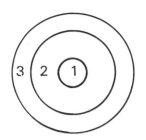

1 Sensibility
2 Understanding
3 Reason

(Cited in Barrett, 1986, p. 86)

Barrett (1986) comments:

> Consider now the widest circle-that part of mind that is concerned with transcendent ideas like God. The intent of diagram is to represent this circle as penetrating the inner circle of sense perception . . . We exist within the question of God. We cannot escape it; it is always there for us, however we may seek to forget or evade it. (p. 87)

Holism attempts to confront the big questions — What is the meaning of existence? What is my role in the universe? How can I view death? Atomism and pragmatism can never adequately address these questions through empiricism or the scientific method.

Specific approaches have been advocated within the perennial philosophy to cultivate intuition. These methods, such as contemplation and meditation, have been developed to help one to "see." Again, this seeing is usually a gradual awakening to the interconnectedness of things.

Emerson, for example, suggested that it was helpful to be quiet and to listen. In this quiet, we can gain access to the "Infinitude" within each person. Gandhi believed that silence was helpful in seeking God. He said: "It (silence) has now become both a physical and spiritual necessity for me. Originally it was taken to relieve the sense of pressure. Then I wanted time for writing. After, however, I had practiced it for some time, I saw the spiritual value of it. It suddenly flashed across my mind that that was the time when I could best hold communication with God. And now I feel as though I was naturally built for silence." (p. 101)

The contemplation of Emerson, however, is different from Gandhi's meditation. In Eastern practices meditation tends to be more focussed (for example, repeating a mantra and counting one's breath) than contemplation, which is more unstructured.

Values Are Derived from Seeing and Realizing the Interconnectedness of Reality

Values are derived from realizing the fundamental connectedness between individuals; in other words, values are linked to relatedness. Positive values enhance or realize that relatedness and negative values foster separateness and paranoia. Caring, for example, is a central value in the perennial philosophy. Heidegger concludes that caring is the "primordial state of being." Noddings (1984) has developed an ethic of caring. Noddings claims that caring is characterized by a receptivity or engrossment, meaning that when we care, we receive the concerns of others. If as teachers we care about our students, then we tend to take on their problems as our own. Noddings claims, ''I can lecture to hundreds, and this neither is consequential nor unimportant, but this is not teaching. To teach involves a giving of self and a receiving of others'' (p. 113).

For Noddings, caring is rooted in a basic relatedness between people (for example, teacher and student), and this relatedness is a fundamental source of joy. In referring to the mother–child relationship, she claims, ''When I look at my child — even one of my grown children — and recognize the fundamental relations in which we are each defined, I often experience a deep and overwhelming joy. It is the recognition of longing for relatedness that forms the foundation of our ethic'' (p. 6)

This relatedness provides the basic context for morality. Noddings is suspicious of abstract rules and formulas as a basis for moral decision-making. She tends to equate analytic and abstract approaches to moral education with masculinity, while a feminine approach to morality has to do with concrete situations in which the individual is concerned with caring and human relatedness.

At the centre of Noddings's approach is what she calls the ethical ideal of caring. She avoids relativism by arguing that caring is the fundamental ethical ideal which sustains us. What is ''right'' is that which helps maintain caring and relatedness.

The Realization of the Fundamental Unity of Existence Leads to Social Action to Counter Injustice and Human Suffering

If human beings realize they are part of a fundamental unity then they naturally feel a connectedness and responsibility to others. However, perennial philosophers are not necessarily social activists. Most important is the idea that social reform would start from within. According to Emerson (1903):

> ''The origin of all reform is in that mysterious foundation of the moral sentiment in man, which, amidst the natural, ever contains the supernatural for men. That is new and creative. That is alive. That alone can make a man other than he is.'' (Vol. 1, p. 272)

Emerson's moral sentiment is analogous to his ''big fellow,'' which is connected to the Oversoul. Although Emerson was not a social activist, he spoke out against slavery and particularly against Daniel Webster's support of the Fugitive Slave law. He also opposed the exclusion of the Cherokee Indians from Georgia and supported women's rights.

Gandhi, of course, was a social activist who used *ahimsa* (non-violence) and *satyagraha* (soul force) as vehicles for social change. For Gandhi (1980), religion and politics cannot be compartmentalized:

> I could not be leading a religious life unless I identified myself with the whole of mankind, and that I could not do unless I took part in politics. The whole gamut of man's activities today constitutes an indivisible whole. You cannot divide social, economic, political and purely religious work into watertight compartments. I do not know any religion apart from human activity. It provides a moral basis to all other activities which they would otherwise lack, reducing life to a maze of ''sound and fury signifying nothing.'' (p. 63)

Holism and Education

Atomism can be linked with competency-based education and pragmatism with inquiry-oriented approaches to curriculum, while holism can be connected to approaches such as confluent education and Waldorf education, which are discussed more fully in the second half of this book.

Holistic programs also facilitate the student's relatedness with the community. Some educators (Noddings, 1984; Newmann, 1975) advocate that the school should encourage student involvement in community service. For example, Noddings suggests that the student have opportunities to practise caring. Students should be assigned to "hospitals, nursing homes, animal shelters, parks and botanical gardens where the primary focus is on developing competence in caring." Newmann's (1975) primary focus is engaging the student in social change as his aim is to develop in the student an ability to effect his or her social environment. Some of the social action projects Newmann advocates include: "telephone conversations, letter writting, participation in meetings, research and study, testifying before public bodies, door-to-door canvassing, fund-raising media production,bargaining and negotiation; and also publicly visible activity associated with the more militant forms" (pp. 54-55).

Conclusion

The atomistic worldview can be seen as a source of alienation because it promotes fragmentation and compartmentalization.

Dewey and Childs also recognize the limitations of the atomistic worldview:

> The assumption implicit in the method of much of the work referred to is that processes and functions with which education deals are isolable, because they are independent of one another. This involves the philosophical notion that character, mental life, experience, and the methods of dealing with them, are composed of separable parts and that there is no whole, no integralness in them, that what seems to be a unity is in reality nothing but an aggregate of parts. This philosophy once dominated physical science. In physics and biology its inadequacy from a scientific point of view is now realized. Yet it has been taken over by that school of educational "science" which denies the importance of a philosophy in conducting education. (p. 289)

But does pragmatism offer a satisfying alternative to atomism? Pragmatic inquiry is an improvement over educational alternatives associated with an atomistic perspective. The universe is no longer a random set of atoms or a closed deterministic system. Instead, pragmatism offers a more optimistic view of experience where the person can act in an intelligent manner. However, there are problems with the pragmatists' model of intelligence. In most cases pragmatic inquiry is what Howard Gardner (1983) calls logical-mathematical intelligence. Gardner argues for a theory of multiple intelligences and claims that pragmatic inquiry dismisses other forms of human experience. Although Dewey bridged the dichotomy of atomism (science and everyday experience), he created a monistic approach to problem-solving. There is little room for nonlinear or holistic forms of thinking and perception in pragmatic inquiry. For example, various forms of intuition are not acknowledged which are so fundamental to both scientific and aesthetic thinking. Einstein claimed that fantasy was critical to the discovery of the theory of relativity. He said: "When I examine myself and my methods of thought I come to the conclusion that the gift of fantasy has meant more to me than my talent for absorbing positive knowledge." Many artists and scientists have reported how imagery is central to the creative process. In general, incubation, intuition, and imagery are not part of pragmatic inquiry or logical-mathematical intelligence.

Another difficulty with pragmatism is that there is no over-reaching unity as we are basically left with problem-solving in indeterminate situations. In other words, our main source of connectedness is through reflective experience. This is not enough, as reflective experience is only a partial connectedness that denies the wholeness of existence. Connectedness that transcends reflective experience can be found in poetry, music, myths, spiritual insight, and these forms are not given adequate scope in pragmatic inquiry. Although Dewey writes of aesthetics, what is missing is a sense of awe and mystery. Einstein (1984) said: "The most beautiful experience we can have is the mysterious. It is the fundamental emotion which stands at the cradle of true art and true science." (p. 40)

Another problem with pragmatic inquiry is the ethical relativism. Values in pragmatism are always rooted in a particular context or problem. We miss, then, transcendent values such as caring (Noddings, 1984). A transcendent value allows humans to feel a fundamental connectedness with others and with the universe. Again in pragmatic inquiry we have a rational cognitive approach to morality. Noddings points out the problems with this form of morality when she says: "a difficulty arises when we approach the teaching of morality of ethical behavior from a rational cognitive approach. We fail to share with each other the feelings, the conflicts, the hopes and ideas that influence our eventual choices. We share only the justification for our acts and not what motivates and touches us." (p. 8)

The model of rational intelligence and pragmatic inquiry leaves us in a spiritual vacuum. We have moved beyond the world of atoms to a world that is dominated by pragmatic inquiry and rational intelligence. One of the reasons for this dominance is Dewey's rejection of Hegelian philosophy (Scheffler, 1974).

> Dewey transforms the Hegelian emphasis on Reason or Spirit into an emphasis on science and its works. Absolute Spirit is replaced, in Dewey's philosophy, by the operation of the scientific intelligence. It is science that develops from problematic stage to problematic stage, unifying progressively the tensions and difficulties that give birth to its motivating questions. It is science, also, that transforms the world through its revision of inherited concepts of nature and practice, setting the stage for new conditions of social life (p. 195).

In atomism there is a fundamental tension between randomness and determinism. In pragmatism there is tension between contextualism and the monism of the scientific method. However, as Scheffler points out, the monism of the scientific method tends to predominate. This is certainly the case in education where pragmatic inquiry models have tended to predominate over more pluralistic approaches to inquiry that include aesthetic and spiritual experience.

Holism, however, overcomes many of the limitations of pragmatism. First, thinking is not reduced to a monistic conception. Divergent approaches to problem-solving are accepted and encouraged through the use of metaphor, imagery, and incubation. Holism, then, tends to avoid reifying procedures; true, procedures or linear methods are employed, but they are usually linked with intuitive methods so their full benefits can be realized. Another important criteria for holistic education and what helps separate it from the other two positions is an acceptance of the wholeness of the child and seeing the child in relation to his or her surroundings. Competency-based education focusses on behavior and inquiry approaches tend to emphasize cognitive processes. The holistic curriculum recognizes these elements but acknowledges a fundamental ground of being of which these elements are a part. In the holistic curriculum the student is not reduced to a set of competencies that must be ''performed,'' or an abstract set of mental processes; instead, there is an acceptance of the richness and wholeness of human experience.

The teacher's wholeness also cannot be ignored. The personal growth of the teacher is central to the holistic curriculum, as you cannot build a ''teacher proof'' holistic curriculum. Instead, the teacher is aware that his or her own consciousness is connected and has an effect on the students' consciousness. The teacher, however, is not a role model in the traditional sense; rather he or she attempts to open more fully to Merton's ''inner self'' and Emerson's ''moral sentiment'' within. In competency-based education the teacher is a trainer, pragmatism a facilitator of inquiry, and in the holistic curriculum a potential source of relatedness and wholeness.

Holism avoids the relativism or pragmatism and the artificial value neutrality of atomism. Values are accepted as having a central role in the curriculum. A value neutral role is not advocated for the school or teacher; instead values and principles that are central to the program are made explicit. The holistic curriulum does not shun controversy. Noddings (1984) claims that ''God, sex, killing, loving, fear, hope, and hate must all be open to discussion . . . It is absurd to suppose that we are educating when we know these matters lies at the very heart of human existence'' (p. 184). In short, the holistic curriculum is not sanitized to remove potential controversy.

The holistic curriculum is not without its problems. First, the perennial philosophy is alienating to some because the language associated with it is not as precise as the language of atomism and logical positivism. Terms such as Oversoul and Universal Mind are attempting to convey something that is beyond concept. In this sense poetry, imagery, music, and spiritual insight are more appropriate vehicles for holism than empiricism and analytic methodologies. In many cases the poetry of Wordsworth or the music of Bach and Mozart can convey more powerfully the harmony of the universe than the prose of Gandhi, Emerson, and Merton.

Because the perennial philosophy is difficult to articulate and thus to understand, holistic programs are often difficult to sustain in schools. Programs such as confluent education are also difficult to evaluate and thus are the first to be attacked in periods of retrenchment. Despite these difficulties, we should remember the paradigmatic roots of the approaches we use in school and the links between these roots and our atomic age. By fragmenting the curriculum we contribute to our disconnectedness; by approaching curriculum from an integrated and interdependent perspective we begin to counter our alienation.

Perhaps what is most appealing in holism is the vision of an interconnected universe of which we are a part. Some examples of this vision have already been presented in this book. A particularly compelling vision of this unity comes from the novelist Mark Helperin in his book *Winter's Tale:*

Nothing is predetermined: it is determined, or was determined, or will be determined. No matter, it all happened at once, in less than an instant, and time was invented because we cannot comprehend in one glance the enormous and detailed canvas that we have been given — so we track it, in linear fashion, piece by piece. Time, however, can be easily overcome; not by chasing the light, but by standing back far enough to see it all at once. The universe is still and complete. Everything that ever was, is; everything that ever will be, is — and so on, in all possible combinations. Though in perceiving it we imagine that it is in motion, and unfinished, it is quite finished and quite astonishingly beautiful. In the end, or rather, as things really are, any event, no matter how small, is intimately and sensibly tied to all others. All rivers run full to the sea; those who are apart are brought together; the lost ones are redeemed; the dead come back to life; the perfectly blue days that have begun and ended in golden dimness continue, immobile and accessible; and, when all is perceived in such a way as to obviate time, justice becomes apparent not as something that will be, but as something that is. (p. 360)

In the holistic worldview we are no longer atomized or confronted with endless problems which can only be resolved through a monistic strategy; instead we are whole. This vision of wholeness can be traced as far back as Pythagoras in the West and is found in most Eastern cultures. It is now being articulated by scientists in such diverse fields as medicine and subatomic physics. Educators should also consider restoring the compelling vision of wholeness as a guiding image for the curriculum.

References

Ayer, A. J. *Philosophy in the Twentieth Century.* New York: Vintage Books, 1984.

Barrett, W. *The Death of the Soul.* Garden City, N.Y.: Anchor Press/Doubleday, 1986.

Barrett, W. *The Illusion of Technique.* New York: Anchor Press, Doubleday, 1979.

Barrett, W. *Irrational Man: A Study in Existential Philosophy.* New York: Doubleday Anchor Books, 1962.

Bobbit, F. *How to Make a Curriculum.* Boston: Houghton Mifflin, 1924.

Brown, G. T. *Human Teaching for Human Learning: An Introduction to Confluent Education.* New York: Viking Press, 1971.

Brown, G. T., Phillips, M., and Shapiro, S. *Getting It All Together: Confluent Education.* Bloomington, Ind.: Phi Delta Kappa Educational Foundation, 1976.

Butler, J. Donald. *Four Philosophies and Their Practice in Education and Religion.* New York: Harper and Row, 1951.

Calkins, M. W. "The philosophical credo of an absolutistic personalist." In *Contemporary American Philosophy,* edited by G. P. Adams and W. P. Montague. 2 Vols. New York: MacMillan, 1930.

Capadli, N.: Kelly, E.; and Navia, L. *An Invitation to Philosophy.* New York: Prometheus Book, 1981.

Clark, R. W. *Einstein the Life and Times.* New York: Avon Books, 1971.

Davies, P. *Superforce: The Search for a Grand Unified Theory of Nature.* New York: Simon and Schuster, 1984.

Dewey, J. *Democracy and Education.* New York: MacMillan/Free Press, 1916, 1966.

Dewey, J. *Experience and Education.* New York: MacMillan/Collier Books, 1938, 1963.

Dewey, J., and Childs, J. L. "The underlying philosophy of education." In *The Educational Frontier,* edited by W. H. Kilpatrick. New York: Century, 1933.

Einstein, A. "Cosmic religious feeling." In *Quantam Questions,* edited by K. Wilber. Boulder, Colorado: Shambhala, 1984.

Einstein, A. *Einstein a Portrait.* Corte Madera, Calif., 1984.

Emerson, R. W. *The Complete Works,* Vol. III. Boston: Houghton Mifflin, 1903-1904.

Emerson, R. W. *Selected Writing.* Edited by W. H. Gilman. New York: New American Library, 1965.

Gandhi, M. *All Men Are Brothers: Autobiographical Reflections.* Edited by Krishna Kripalani. New York: Continuum, 1980.

Gardner, H. *Frames of Mind.* New York: Basic Books, 1983.

Heisenberg, W. "The Debate between Plato and Democritus." In *Quantam Questions,* edited by K. Wilber. Boulder, Colorado: Shambhala, 1984.

Helperin, Mark. *Winter's Tale.* New York: Harcourt, Brace, Jovanovich, 1983.

Hunt, I., and Draper, W. W. *Lightning in His Hand: The Life Story of Nicola Tesla.* Hawthorne, Ca.: Omni Publications, 1964.

Joyce, B., and Weil, M. *Models of Teaching.* 2nd ed. Englewood Cliffs, N.J.: Prentice Hall, 1980.

Kaplan, A. *The New World of Philosophy.* New York: Random House, 1961.

Lavine, T. Z. *From Socrates to Sartre: The Philosophic Quest.* New York: Bantam Books, 1984.

Massialas, B. G., Sprague, N. F., and Hurst, J. B. *Social Issues Through Inquiry.* Englewood Cliffs, N.J.: Prentice Hall, 1975.

McAshan, H. H. *Competency-Based Education and Behavioral Objectives.* Englewood Cliffs, N.J.: Educational Technology Publications, 1979.

Merton, T. "The Inner Experience." Unpublished manuscript, fourth draft, 1959.

Needleman, J. *The Heart of Philosophy.* New York: Alfred A. Knopf, 1982.

Newmann, F. W. *Education for Citizen Action: Challenge for Secondary Curriculum.* Berkeley, Ca.: McCutchan, 1975.

Noodings, N. *Caring: A Feminine Approach to Ethics and Moral Education.* Berkeley, Ca.: University of California Press, 1984.

Sacheffler, I. *Four Pragmatists: A Critical Introduction to Peirce, James, Mead, and Dewey.* New York: Humanities Press, 1974.

Schon, D. A. *The Reflective Practitioner: How Professionals Think in Action.* New York: Basic Books, 1983.

Schroedinger, E. "Why not Talk Physics," In *Quantam Questions,* edited by K. Wilber. Boulder, Colorado: Shambhala, 1984.

Skinner, B. F. *The Technology of Teaching.* New York: Appleton Century Crofts, 1984.

Tanner, D., and Tanner, L. *Curriculum Development: Theory into Practice.* New York: MacMillan, 1980.

Teilhard de Chardin, P. *The Divine Milieu.* New York: Harper and Row, 1968.

2

The Psychological Context: The Transpersonal Self

Behavioral (atomistic-transmission) psychology is based on the physical self; cognitive (pragmatic-transactive) psychology is based in the mind; transpersonal (holistic-transformational) psychology is based in the Self. What is the Self? I will be examining this question in depth, but for the present I shall follow Huston Smith's (1982) definition:

> Unconsciously dwelling at our inmost center; beneath the surface shuttlings of our sensations, percepts, and thoughts; wrapped in the envelope of soul (which too is finally porous) is the eternal and the divine, the final Reality: not soul, not personality, but All-Self beyond all selfishness; spirit enwombed in matter and wrapped round with psychic traces. Within every phantom-self dwells this divine; within all creatures incarnate sleeps the Infinite Sentence — unevolved, hidden, unfelt, unknown, yet destined from all eternity to waken at last and, tearing away the ghostly web of sensuous mind, break forever its chrysalis of flesh and pass beyond all space and time. (p. 51)

Smith also refers to the Self as the Sacred Unconscious; Buddhists call it our Buddha-nature; Hindus use the term *Atman*; Christ said, "the Kingdom of God is within you"; and Psychosynthesis refers to our Transpersonal Self. The Self is the deepest part of being which at the same time is connected to the highest principle of the universe — God, or the Tao. In Hinduism there is the reference to the Atman (individual consciousness)–Brahman (universal consciousness) connection. Before examining the Self in more detail, I shall review briefly the three positions and their psychologies. This is done in the form of a chart:

Position	Psychology	Location	Focus
Transmission	Behavioral	Body	Behavior
Transaction	Cognitive	Mind	Intelligence
Transformation	Transpersonal	Self	Wisdom

Behavioral psychology ignores the inner life of the person and is only concerned with environment and behavior. Stimuli and reinforcements are designed to influence how a person acts; for example, positive reinforcement is used to increase the frequency of a particular behavior while negative reinforcement is designed to decrease the frequency of a behavior.

Cognitive psychology treats of cognition and intelligence. In most cases, it has focussed on what Gardner (1984) calls mathematical-logical intelligences. Logical-mathematical intelligence is what Piaget studied in his own work. Gardner refers to six other intelligences, but they are still within the domain of pragmatic psychology. No mention is made of spiritual intelligence or wisdom, which is one of the main goals of transpersonal psychology. Wisdom is intelligence rooted in the Self. Wisdom links intuition and intelligence in order to deal with the large questions: What is our role in the universe? How can I deal with human suffering?

Transpersonal psychology has two sources. One source is the mystical traditions within the major faiths — Christianity, Buddhism, Islam, Hinduism, and Judaism. The other source includes psychologies such as Jungian psychology and psychosynthesis, which have a spiritual element. I shall now turn to the conceptions of the Self within the major spiritual traditions.

Christianity

Jesus continually referred to the Kingdom of God; but what are the characteristics of this kingdom? Jesus used parables to elaborate on the meaning of this kingdom. He said:

> The kingdom of heaven is like treasure hidden in a field which someone has found; he hides it again, goes off happy, sells everything he owns and buys the field. (Matthew 13:44)

The kingdom, then, is something that is discovered within (Luke 17:21). In order to discover it one needs to see in a certain way. One needs to drop all conditioning and become like a child (Mark 9:35-37). Jesus was critical of the Pharisees, who followed elaborate rules and laws; instead, he advocated a radical awakening. He said:

> For I tell you, if your virtue goes no deeper than that of the Scribes and Pharisees, you will never get into the kingdom of heaven. (Matthew 5:20)

Here, Jesus is clearly referring to profound inner transformation. Once this transformation has begun he compares the growth of Self (the Kingdom of God) to other images of growth:

> The kingdom of heaven is like a mustard seed which a man took and sowed in his field. It is the smallest of all the seeds, but when it has grown it is the biggest shrub of all and becomes a tree so that the birds of the air come and shelter in its branches. (Matthew 13:31-32; Mark 4:30-32; Luke 13:18-19)

> The kingdom of heaven is like the yeast a woman took and mixed in with three measures of flour till it was leavened all through. (Matthew 13:33; Luke 13:20-21)

When realized within us the Kingdom of God leads to wholeness. Jesus often said "your faith has made you whole."

Different mystics and sages have elaborated on Jesus' conception of the kingdom within us. Augustine, Eckhart, Teresa of Avila, John Wesley, and Thomas Merton are among the few who have referred to our spiritual centre. They have called it the soul, the eye of the soul, the ground of the soul, the ground of being, the heart, the transcendental Self (McNamara, 1975). Generally, Christians hold that our Self is not God, but the point within us where God touches us. In other words, it is where we and God meet.

Merton (1959) develops the concept of the Self in an unpublished manuscript called "The Inner Experience." He calls it the inner self and contrasts it to our ego, or what Merton calls the exterior "I". He says:

> But the exterior "I", the "I" of projects, of temporal finalities, the "I" that manipulates objects in order to take possession of them, is alien from the hidden, interior "I" who has no projects and seeks to accomplish nothing, even contemplation. He seeks only to be, and to move (for he is dynamic) according to the secret laws of Being itself, and according to the promptings of a Superior Freedom (that is, of God), rather than to plan and to achieve according to his own desires . . . (pp. 4-5)

In contrast, the inner self of "I" is characterized by the capacity for the deepest connection with others:

> . . . The inner "I" is certainly the sanctuary of our most personal and individual solitude, and yet, paradoxically, it is precisely that which is most solitary and personal in ourselves which is united with the "Thou" who confronts us. We are not capable of union with one another on the deepest level until the inner self in each one of us is sufficiently awakened to confront the inmost spirit of the other. (p. 20)

How can we awaken the inner self? Merton suggests that we can awaken the inner self through contemplation and love. He also argues that the two are closely related:

> . . . In fact, contemplation is man's highest and most essential spiritual activity. It is his most creative and dynamic affirmation of his divine sonship . . .

> . . . Solitude is necessary for spiritual freedom. But once that freedom is acquired, it demands to be put to work in the service of a love in which there is no longer subjection or slavery. Mere withdrawal, without the return to freedom in action, would lead to a static and death-like inertia of the spirit in which the inner self would not awaken at all. (p. 22)

Merton, then, refers to a balance between contemplation and service to others. If we become too inward oriented, we lose touch with others; if we become too caught up in the external world, then we can become lost in the exterior "I" and delusions of our ego.

Judaism

The transpersonal self is also found within Judaism. When Moses saw the burning bush on Mt. Horeb he encountered his Self through God's self revelation:

> And Moses said unto God: "Behold when I come unto the children of Israel,

and shall say unto them: The God of your fathers hath sent me unto you; and they shall say to me: What is His name? what shall I say unto them?'' And God said unto Moses: ''I AM THAT I AM''; and He said: ''Thus shalt thou say unto the children of Israel: I AM hath sent me unto you.'' (Exodus 3:13-14)

The I AM is another name for our centre or Self.

There is also an ancient mystical strand within Judaism known as the Kabbalah (Hoffman, 1980) which acknowledges that there is a part within us that is connected to the Divine. The Kabbalah states that there are three aspects to each person: (1) *nefesh*, a type of biological energy; (2) the *ruah*, or spirit, which is another name for the individual's psyche; and (3) *neshamah,* or the Self, which unites the person with the universal divine essence. The Kabbalah recommends techniques similar to various eastern spiritual practices in the attempt to reach unity with the Self. For example, according to Scholem (1961), Abraham Abulafia, the Kabbalist of the thirteenth century, advocated Yogic postures, breathing exercises, and meditation. Other Kabbalistic practices have involved the recitation of special rhythmic prayers that are similar to Hindu mantras. For example, it is recommended that the person meditate on the inner sound of *Aleph,* the first letter of the Hebrew alphabet. This exercise is quite similar to the Aum meditation in Hinduism.

Buddhism

Buddhism posits that our selves or egos are an illusion; instead, Buddhists refer to our Buddha-nature. Bodhidarma, the Indian Buddhist sage who brought Buddhism to China in the sixth century A.D. said: ''If you wish to seek the Buddha, you ought to see into your own Nature for this Nature is the Buddha himself'' (cited in Suzuki, 1955, p. 87). As in the other spiritual traditions, the person needs to look inwards. Bodhidarma said: ''If, instead of seeing into your own Nature, you turn away to seek the Buddha in external things, you will never get at him.'' (Suzuki, p. 88)

Chih, a Chinese Buddhist monk of the eighth century A.D., described one's true self in this way: ''This Nature is from the first pure and undefiled, serene and undisturbed. It belongs to no categories of duality such as being and non-being, pure and defiled, long and short, taking in and giving up; the Body remains in its suchness. To have a clear insight into this is to see one's Self-nature. Therefore, seeing into one's Self-nature is becoming the Buddha.'' (Cited in Suzuki, 1956, p. 206)

Chogyam Trungpa (1984) described this Buddha-nature as a basic goodness. He says: ''Every human being has a basic nature of goodness, which is undiluted and unconfused. That goodness contains tremendous gentleness and appreciation'' (p. 30). Trungpa goes on to describe how this goodness can unfold:

> The basic point is that, when you live your life in accordance with basic goodness, then you develop natural elegance. Your life can be spacious and relaxed, without having to be sloppy. You can actually let go of your depression and embarrassment about being a human being, and you can cheer up. You don't have to blame the world for your problems. You can relax and appreciate the world (p. 32)

How can we access this basic goodness? Again meditation is the main vehicle.

Our life is an endless journey; it is like a broad highway that extends infinitely into the distance. The practice of meditation provides a vehicle to travel on that road. Our journey consists of constant ups and downs, hope and fear, but it is a good journey. The practice of meditation allows us to experience all the textures of the roadway, which is what the journey is all about. Through the practice of meditation, we begin to find that within ourselves there is no fundamental complaint about anything or anyone at all. (p. 84)

Hinduism

As mentioned earlier, Hinduism discusses the connection between individual and universal consciousness as Atman-Brahman. The Purpose of spiritual practice is to discover the Atman within oneself. When this is done, union with Brahman is also realized. Krishna in the *Bhagavad Gita* describes the Atman in the following manner:

Know this Atman
Unborn, undying,
Never ceasing,
Never beginning,
Deathless, birthless,
Unchanging for ever.
How can It die
The death of the body?

Knowing It birthless,
Knowing It deathless,
Knowing It endless,
For ever unchanging,
Dream not you do
The deed of the killer,
Dream not the power
Is yours to command it.

Worn-out garments
Are shed by the body:
Worn-out bodies
Are shed by the dweller

Within the body.
New bodies are donned
By the dweller, like garments.

Not wounded by weapons,
Not burned by fire,
Not dried by the wind,
Not wetted by water:
Such is the Atman,

Not dried, not wetted,
Not burned, not wounded,
Innermost element,
Everywhere, always,
Being of beings,
Changeless, eternal,
For ever and ever.

(Cited in Johnson, 1971, pp. 56-57)

How does one realize the Atman? The Veda — the mystic literature of Hinduism — describes four methods by which a person can attain union (yoga) with God.

One yoga is *karma yoga.* Karma yoga is the path of selfless service where we offer the fruits of our work to God. In one's daily life the person offers his work to God and thus becomes pure in heart.

Jnana yoga is the way to God realized through the intellect. The person learns to discriminate between the Eternal and the non-eternal, and to focus his or her life on the Eternal, thereby realizing the Atman within.

The path of devotion is *Bakhti yoga.* People who follow this path fill their hearts with love for the Divine. For example, the devotee may repeat the name of God in order to merge with the Divine.

Raja yoga is a fourth path where the individual concentrates on meditation as the means for achieving union. Here the yogi develops one-pointedness of mind so that he or she can concentrate fully on God.

It is possible that a yogi may use all these methods, but probably he or she will concentrate on one method as the main vehicle for union. The choice will depend to some extent on the temperament of the yogi.

Islam

To examine the Self in Islam I would like to turn to Sufism, which is the mystic form of the Islamic faith. Sufism was a reaction to over-intellectualism and legalism in some forms of Islam. Sufism claims that God can be experienced by light, knowledge, and love. Divine union, or "Tawhid" has two main stages: (1) "Fana", or the extinction of the ego; and (2) "Ba'qa", or reintegration in God. Al-Ghazali, the Islamic theologian of the twelfth century, made Sufism more acceptable within orthodox Islam. Jalaudin Rumi, the thirteenth-century Sufi, was a famous poet who also founded the Melvlevi order of "whirling dervishes." The dervish uses the dance as well as repeating the Name of God, Allah, to realize Self. Rumi said this about the search for God:

> Cross and Christians, end to end, I examined. He was not on the Cross. I went to the Hindu temple, to the ancient pagoda. In none of them was there any sign. To the uplands of Herat I went, and to Kandahar. I looked. He was not on the heights or in the lowlands. Resolutely, I went to the summit of the (fabulous) mountain of Kaf. There only was the dwelling of the (legendary) Anqu bird. I went to the Kaaba of Mecca. He was not there. I asked about him from Avicenna, the philosopher. He was beyond the range of Avicenna . . . I looked into my own heart. In that place, I saw him. He was in no other place. (Shah, 1970, p. 105)

One of the main ways to Wisdom for the Sufi is storytelling. The following story is a metaphorical description of awakening to the Self (e.g. the Jewel):

THE PRECIOUS JEWEL

> All wisdom, according to Daudzadah, is contained in the various levels of interpretation of this ancient traditional tale.
>
> In a remote realm of perfection, there was a just monarch who had a wife and a wonderful son and daughter. They all lived together in happiness.
>
> One day the father called his children before him and said:
>
> "The time has come, as it does for all. You are to go down, an infinite distance, to another land. You shall seek and find and bring back a precious Jewel."
>
> The travelers were conducted in disguise to a strange land, whose inhabitants almost all lived a dark existence. Such was the effect of this place that the two lost touch with each other, wandering as if asleep.
>
> From time to time they saw phantoms, similitudes of their country and of the Jewel, but such was their condition that these things only increased the depth of their reveries, which they now began to take as reality.

When news of his children's plight reached the king, he sent word by a trusted servant, a wise man:

"Remember your mission, awaken from your dream, and remain together."

With this message they roused themselves, and with the help of their rescuing guide they dared the monstrous perils which surrounded the Jewel, and by its magic aid returned to their realm of light, there to remain in increased happiness for evermore.

I. Shah, *Thinkers of the East* (London: Jonathan Cape, 1971) p. 176.

Religions and the Self

This review of how the major faiths articulate their conception of the Self is not an attempt to gloss over differences in conceptions. Even within the various faiths there are disputes about the nature of the person and his or her relationship to God. For example, in Christianity the monastic and contemplative traditions have not been predominant. Yet there do appear to be more similarities than differences among the mystical strains of the faiths. And from these commonalities arises the core of the perennial philosophy. This core acknowledges the importance of our centre or Buddha nature and outlines various methods to reach the Self.

Psychology and the Self

I shall now examine various psychologies and their description of the Self.

Jung

Jung's conception of the Self is diagrammed below (Samuels and Samuels, 1975, p. 72):

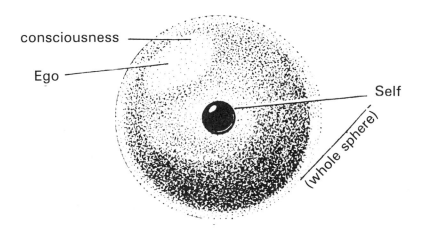

The ego is seen as a small illuminated area in the larger, dark sphere of the psyche. The ego is the individual's conscious awareness that views the images which come from both within the psyche and without. The Self or soul lies at the centre of the psyche and is the "inventor, organizer, and source of dream images" (Jung, 1968, p. 161). The Self is also the source of spiritual insight and is connected with Jung's notion of the collective unconscious. Jung suggests that the Self can send images to the ego and that these images are important to the person's spiritual development. Thus the person needs to turn inward to hear the messages of the Self. Jung (1933) suggests that an image can surface when an individual is confronting a problem or provide inspiration for artistic activity.

Psychosynthesis

Robert Assagioli, the founder of psychosynthesis, articulated the concept of the Higher or Transpersonal Self. Below is a diagram of Assagioli's (Ferrucci, 1982, p. 44) conception of consciousness:

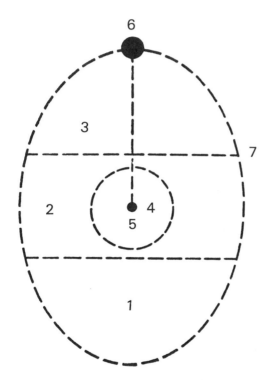

1. "Lower" unconscious
2. Middle unconscious
3. Superconscious
4. Field of consciousness
5. Personal self, or "I"
6. Transpersonal Self
7. Collective unconscious

The lower unconscious represents the person's psychological past in terms of repressions and distant memories. Psychosynthesis attempts to tap these memories and repressions. If they are ignored the repressed energy can lead to neurosis and dysfunction.

The middle unconscious (2) is our present state of mind and is applied to our field of consciousness (4). Our field of consciousness is what we perceive at the present moment.

Our potential future is represented by the superconscious (3). Here we receive our highest intuitions and inspirations — "artistic, philosophical or scientific, ethical imperatives and urges to humanitarian and heroic action. It is the source of higher feelings, such as altruistic love; of genius and the states of contemplation, illumination and ecstacy.'' (Assagioli, 1965, pp. 17-18).

These three levels of consciousness can be viewed in a developmental or evolutionary sense where the lower unconscious is seen as an early stage of development and the superconscious as a more evolved form of awareness. Assagioli was influenced by Jung and saw the individual psyche surrounded by the collective unconscious (7). All individuals, then, are connected through this collectivity.

Assagioli makes the distinction between our personal self and our Transpersonal Self. The former is our ego which is defined by our personal desires and our social role. The Transpersonal Self, however, is not bound by personal ambition but has a holistic vision that connects the psyche with the universal.

Psychosynthesis has developed a number of techniques to work with different parts of the psyche. Piero Ferrucci (1982) describes a number of these techniques in *What We May Be*. One of the techniques is visualization. Below is one example:

THE DIAMOND

Vividly imagine a diamond.

See all its shining facets, perfectly integrated into one whole.

See the perfection of its shape.

Hold the diamond in front of your inner eye, and let yourself be pervaded by its crystalline beauty.

The word ''diamond'' comes from the Greek *adamas*, ''unconquerable.'' As you identify with this diamond, sense it connecting you to that part of you which is likewise unconquerable, your Self.

Your Self is unconquerable by fear, by obscurity, by the pulls and the pushes of everyday conditioning. It is untouched by the shadows of the past, the monsters of worry, the phantoms of the future, the demons of greed, the dictatorship of social conformity. It is your very essence, shining through innumerable facets and yet one. Realize that you are that Self, and, as the image of the diamond fades away, let this sense of Self strengthen and grow ever clearer in you. (pp. 123-24)

Other exercises include identifying one's subpersonalities and dialoguing with these personalities; disidentification with subpersonalities; dialoguing with one's inner guide, or Self; working with one's will; focussing attention on and contemplating ideal qualities (for example, joy, gratitude, love, and so on). Some of these techniques will be described more fully in the second part of this book.

Ken Wilber

Ken Wilber has become one of the principal figures in transpersonal psychology. His output has been voluminous and has produced changes in his conception of the Self. In an early article, ''Psychologia Perennis: The Spectrum of Consciousness'' in the *Journal of Transpersonal Psychology* (1975), he described what he called a spectrum of consciousness (see the figure on page 38):

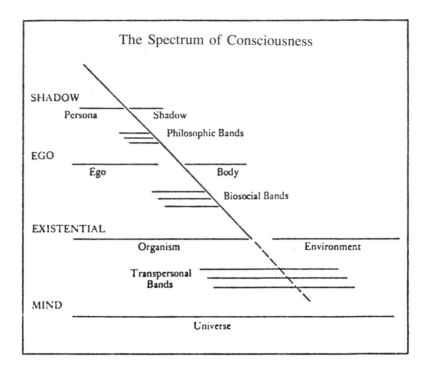

The Spectrum of Consciousness

The spectrum conveys a conception of depth and as one penetrates the levels the Self is realized. In his later work, the focus is more on hierarchical growth where one develops through stages and the Self is realized through this progression. First, however, let's examine his spectrum in more detail.

At the deepest level of mind, consciousness is identical to the reality of the universe; in other words, consciousness and the universe are one. Edwin Schroedinger, the founder of quantum mechanics, describes this level of consciousness:

> That there is only one thing and that what seems to be a plurality is merely a series of different aspects of this one thing, produced by a deception; the same illusion is produced in a gallery of mirrors, and in the same way Gaurisankar and Mt. Everest turned out to be the same peak seen from different valleys . . . Inconceivable as it seems to ordinary reason, you — and all other conscious beings as such — are all in all. Hence this life of yours you are living is not merely a piece of the entire existence, but is in a certain sense the whole . . . (Cited in Wilber, 1975, p. 103)

Next are the transpersonal bands of consciousness that exist between the mind level and the existential level. This reality of state of consciousness exists as a transition between experiencing oneself as a separate organism and experiencing the oneness of phenomena.

At the existential level, the individual is identified with his or her psychophysical organism as it exists in space and time. He or she can experience a sense of wholeness as an organism as well as the ability to discriminate rationally and exercise will. At this level the individual can also experience the biosocial bands, where he or she experiences himself or herself as part of a cultural and social reality; his identity centres around his or her family and cultural ties. This is called the biosocial band because social realities are interjected onto the biological organism.

At the ego level the individual's consciousness/reality is not identified with the physical organism but with his or her self-image. Thus, the organism is split into his psychological make up and his body; in fact, at this level the two become alienated from one another. In other words, an individual would say "I have a body" rather than "I am a body."

Under some circumstances the individual may narrow his or her identity to only part of the ego. Thus, his or her reality becomes associated with a narrow band of consciousness that focusses on an impoverished and inaccurate self-image. This is defined as the shadow level of consciousness.

Each level of consciousness/reality represents an increasingly narrowed sphere of identity from the universe to organism, from organism to ego, and from ego to a part of the ego. Each level of consciousness narrows or broadens depending on its evolutionary state.

Different modes of therapy and education can correspond to the level of consciousness. For example, ego-level therapies attempt to integrate alienated aspects of the ego. Thus, these therapies may focus on healing the split between the ego consciousness and unconsciousness, as in psychoanalysis or various ego psychologies (for example, Erickson, Horney, and so on). Educational approaches at this level include values clarification, Glasser's classroom meeting model, and role-playing, which attempt to develop a positive student self-concept.

Wilber's Levels of Consciousness

Level of consciousness	Educational strategy	Overall aim of strategy
Ego	Role playing, values clarification, Glasser classroom meeting	Positive self-image
Existential	Movement, confluent education, awareness training	Integration of mind and body
Biosocial	Social literacy training	Social awareness & social activity
Transpersonal	Dreamwork, visualization witness	Ego-transcendence
Mind	Meditation	Oneness

Existential level therapies attempt to integrate ego with the organism. The aim is not so much to develop an accurate self-image as to be a total organism. As stated by Perls, "the aim is to extend the boundary of what you accept as yourself to include all organic activities." (Wilber, p. 116)

Such therapies as existential psychology, Gestalt therapy, bioenergetics, hatha yoga, structural integration, and sensory awareness focus on this level. In education we focus on this level when we use confluent education (chapter 7), movement education (chapter 6), and various awareness activities that let students get in touch with themselves.

At the biosocial band, work is done to make one aware of one's social environmental context. Thus, certain family therapies and those that focus on language function at this level. In education, the work of Freire could be seen to apply at this level. Freire describes an approach to education where the individual becomes aware of his social environment and then gains skills in working with this environment to become more autonomous and less oppressed. Alschuler's work in social literacy (chapter 8) could also be seen to apply at this level.

Transpersonal band therapies focus on letting the individual transcend his or her separateness and see problems as one might view clouds floating through the sky or water rushing in the stream. These approaches help the individual to disidentify with his ego trips and cultural realities. Again, the witness is used in transpersonal therapies to facilitate this process.

Psychosynthesis makes use of the witness and disidentification practices to facilitate the transition from the ego to the transpersonal. In education, teachers who employ centring techniques — dream analysis and study of myth — would be functioning in the transpersonal band.

At the level of mind, therapies go beyond dualism to facilitate a oneness with the universe. Here there is no sense of an inner self looking at the outer world; these two worlds are now one and are understood to have never been separate. Approaches that facilitate this level of consciousness include different forms of meditation (chapter 9).

In his more recent work Wilber presents a developmental model of consciousness. Figure 1 on page 41 compares Wilber's model of development with the models developed by Maslow, Kohlberg, and Piaget.

ARCHAIC LEVEL. At the base of development is what Wilber calls the archaic level. The focus on this stage is on physical sensation and emotional, sexual energy. According to Wilber, people operating at this level are dominated by their physical needs. The archaic level is parallel to Maslow's physiological-need level and Kohlberg's stage-one morality level that is organized around punishment and obedience.

MAGICAL LEVEL. At this stage of development, the person begins to think instead of just reacting to physical needs. This stage parallels Piaget's pre-operational stage, Maslow's safety-needs stage, and Kohlberg's stage-two morality level, which is based on egocentric needs.

MYTHIC LEVEL. At this level, the person begins what Piaget calls concrete operational thinking; that is, he or she can figure things out without being deceived by appearances. However, the child at this level cannot reason abstractly (hypothetico-deductive reasoning). This stage corresponds to Maslow's belongingness-needs stage and Kohlberg's conventional morality stage (stages 3 and 4). In general, the person at this level is oriented toward conformity in his or her personal relations.

RATIONAL LEVEL. Here the person is capable of abstract thinking and also can hypothesize and then rationally examine the variables which may or may not support the hypothesis. Thus, the person at the rational stage has entered Piaget's stage of formal operations. This stage correlates with Kohlberg's post-conventional morality stage and Maslow's self-esteem-needs stage.

WILBER	MASLOW	KOHLBERG	PIAGET
Causal			
Subtle	Self-transcendence		
Psychic	Self-actualization	Self-chosen ethical principles	
Rational	Self-esteem	Social-contract position	Formal operations
Mythic	Belongingness	Conventional morality stages 3-4	Concrete operations
Magical	Safety needs	Egocentric orientation	Pre-operations
Archaic	Physiological needs	Punishment orientation	Sensori-motor

Figure1/ Comparison of Wilber's Maslow's, Kohlberg's and Paiget's Development Models

Many hierarchies of development end at this point. However, transpersonal psychologists suggest that the individual is capable of higher levels of consciousness. Wilber (1983) believes that it is reasonable to speculate in this way about the evolution of human consciousness:

> The point is that the general concept of evolution continuing beyond its present stage into some legitimately trans-rational structures is not a totally outrageous notion. Look at the course of evolution to date: from amoebas to humans! Now what if that ratio, amoeba-to-human, were applied to future evolution? That is, amoebas are to humans as humans are to — What? Is it ridiculous to suggest that the "what" might indeed be omega, geist, supermind, spirit? (p. 24)

Based on his study of mystical psychologies, Wilber has developed three stages beyond the rational.

PSYCHIC LEVEL. This is the first stage beyond the rational level. The psychic level goes beyond the rational level by forming networks of conceptual relationships. At this level, the person moves toward a higher order synthesizing ability and makes "connections, relates truths, coordinates ideas, integrating concepts" (Wilber, 1983, p. 27). This stage culminates in what Aurobindo (n.d.) calls the "higher mind." This level "can freely express itself in single ideas, but its most characteristic movement is a mass ideation, a system of totality of truth-seeing at a single view; the relations of idea with idea, of truth with truth, self-seen in the integral whole" (Aurobindo, quoted in Wilber, 1983, p. 27). This stage is parallel to Maslow's self-actualization stage. Wilber (1983) suggests persons at this stage can also experience insight and even illumination — "a type of vision, noeticism, numinous, inspiring, often enstatic, occasionally ecstatic" (p. 29).

SUBTLE LEVEL. At this level, the person experiences what Maslow calls self-transcendence. According to Wilber, the disciplines and insights of the great saints reflect this level of development. At this level, the person experiences the highest level of intuition, that which is not emotionalism or some form of hunch, but direct spiritual insight.

CAUSAL LEVEL. This is the highest level of transpersonal development. Wilber (1983) states: "Passing full through the state of cessation or unmanifest absorption, consciousness is said finally to re-awaken to its absolutely prior and eternal abode as spirit, radiant and all-pervading, one and many, only and all" (pp. 30-31). Here the person becomes identified with Tillich's "Ground of Being" or Spinoza's "Eternal Substance." At this level, one does not have a particular set of experiences, but transcends his or her identity as the "experiencer." Thus, subject–object duality is transcended. Wilber (1983) labels individuals at this level as sages, drawing a distinction between saints and sages:

> As an example of the distinction between subtle saints and causal sages, we may take the Mosaic and Christic epiphanies. The Mosaic revelation on Mt. Sinai has all the standard features of a subtle level apprehension: a numinous Other that is Light, Fire, Insight, and Sound (shabd). Nowhere, however, does Moses claim to be one with or identical with that Being . . . Christ, on the other hand, does claim that "I and the Father are one," a perfect Atmic or causal level apprehension. (pp. 31-32)

In one of his works, Wilber (1983) discusses a framework that is compatible to the one presented in this book. He suggests that there are three levels of knowing which correspond to three positions outlined in this book. Wilber claims that three basic ways of knowing include sensorimotor cognition (body), mental-conceptual thought (mind), and intuition (spirit). These categories parallel the chart given at the beginning of the chapter. The first mode of knowing, which Wilber calls the eye of the flesh, can be linked with the transmission position and atomism.

The mind is the eye of reason and participates in a world of ideas, logic, and concepts. This mode of knowing can be linked with the transaction position and pragmatism.

Finally, the spirit is the source of intuition and contemplation. Again spirit resides in the Self and can be accessed by various forms of meditation. Spirit-intuition can be linked with the transformation position and holism.

Frances Vaughn

Frances Vaughn is a psychotherapist who has written extensively on transpersonal issues. Recently, she has written a book that deals extensively with the transpersonal self (Vaughn, 1986). She argues, like Wilber, that there are several levels of existence — physical, emotional, mental, existential, and spiritual — and that we have identities associated with each level. The transpersonal self is linked with the spiritual level. Vaughn (1986) draws the following distinction between the transpersonal Self and the Super-Ego:

Super-Ego	Transpersonal Self
Judgmental	Compassionate
Fearful	Loving
Opinionated	Wise
Intrusive	Receptive
Dominating	Allowing
Limited	Unlimited
Rationalizing	Intuitive
Controlled	Spontaneous
Restrictive	Creative
Conventional	Inspired
Anxious	Peaceful
Defensive	Open
Separated	Connected

(pp. 42-43)

Vaughn suggests that the transpersonal Self can be accessed through disidentification with the ego, meditation, and visualization. She suggests the following exercise to realize the Self, and her exercise provides an appropriate conclusion to this chapter.

Dialogues with the Transpersonal Self

Each of us has within us a source of wisdom, compassion, and creativity that we can learn to contact.

Imagine that your transpersonal Self represents the highest qualities that you value. This image of your Self embodies all the positive qualities that are latent within you and that you might expect to find in an enlightened being. It embodies your intuitive knowing, your inner wisdom, and your loving kindness. If you were to visibly embody these qualities, how would you see yourself?

Let the image go now, and focus attention on your breathing. When your mind is quiet and your body relaxed, imagine that you are walking alone in a beautiful place where you feel perfectly safe. Reflect on your life as it is and consider any problem that may be troubling you. Pick one issue that you are concerned about and formulate a single question on which you would like to receive guidance.

Imagine now that your transpersonal Self has come to meet you where you are. Take a moment to imagine what it feels like to be in the presence of a being of total compassion. You can ask this being whatever you want to know. Whatever answer is given, listen and take time to reflect on it. It may be exactly what you need to know for the next step on your way. Trust your Self. Become your Self. Let go, say goodbye, and return to being here now in your ordinary waking state. (pp. 56-57)

References

Assagioli, R. *Psychosynthesis.* New York: Viking, 1971.

Ferrucci, P. *What We May Be.* Los Angeles, Calif.: Tarcher, 1982.

Gardner, H. *Frames of Mind.* New York: Basic Books, 1983.

Hoffman, E. "The Kabbalah." *Journal of Humanistic Psychology* 20 (1980), 33-47.

Johnson, C., ed. *Vedanta.* New York: Bantam, 1971.

Jung, C. *Man and His Symbols.* Garden City, New York: Doubleday and Co., 1968.

Jung, C. *Modern Man in Search of a Soul.* New York: Harcourt, Brace, and World, Inc., 1983.

McNamara, W. "Psychology and the Christian Mystical Tradition." In *Transpersonal Psychologies,* edited by C. Tart. New York: Harper & Row, 1975.

Merton, T. "The Inner Experience." Unpublished (four drafts at Thomas Merton Studies Center, Louisville, Ky.), 1959.

Samuels, M., and Samuels, N. *Seeing with the Mind's Eye.* New York: Random House, 1975.

Scholem, G. G. *Major Trends in Jewish Mysticism.* New York: Schochen, 1961.

Shah, I. *The Dermis Probe.* London: Jonathan Cape, 1970; New York: Dutton, 1971.

Shah, I. *Thinkers of the East.* London: Jonathan Cape, 1971.

Smith, H. *Beyond the Post-Modern Mind.* New York: Crossroads, 1982.

Suzuki, D. T. *Zen Buddhism.* Edited by W. Barrett. Garden City, New York: Doubleday, 1956.

Trungpa, C. *Shambhala: The Sacred Path of the Warrior.* Boston: Shambhala, 1984.

Vaughn, F. *The Inward Arc: Healing and Wholeness in Psychotherapy and Spirituality.* Boston: Shambhala, 1986.

Wilber, K. ''Psychologia Perennis: The Spectrum of Consciousness.'' *Journal of Transpersonal Psychology* 7 (1975), 105-132.

Wilber, K. *The Atman Project.* Wheaton, Ill.: Theosophical Publishing House, 1980.

Wilber, K. *A Sociable God.* New York: McGraw-Hill, 1983.

3

The Social Context:
An Ecological/Interdependent
Perspective

We have tended to think acontextually in education; that is, we have not linked the school curriculum to the surrounding social milieu. One of the assumptions of this book is that a particular curriculum approach can often be linked with a parallel social context. The following links can be made with regard to the three positions: transmission position — laissez faire economic theory; transaction position — rational planning; transformation position — an ecological approach. In this chapter I would like to refer briefly to the first two positions and then outline the transformation perspective in more detail.

Transmission Position and Laissez-Faire Economics

Atomistic economics is found in Adam Smith's laissez-faire approach where individuals compete in the market place. The market is the regulating mechanism for setting the price and quality of goods. Heilbroner (1960) has described the atomistic world of Smith very well:

> The world of Adam Smith has been called a world of atomistic competition; a world in which no agent of the productive mechanism, on the side of labor or capital, was powerful enough to interfere with or to resist the pressures of competition. It was a world in which each agent was forced to scurry after its self-interest in a vast social free-for-all. (p. 56)

Milton Friedman has picked up the banner of Smith when he claims that "In its simplest form, such a society consists of a number of independent households — a collection of Robinson Crusoes, as it were" (p. 13). For Friedman the principal link for these individuals is the market place. Friedman (Friedman & Friedman, 1980) argues that "the key insight of Adam Smith's *Wealth of Nations* is misleadingly simple: if an exchange between two parties is voluntary, it will not take place unless both believe they will benefit from it'' (p. 13). One of the problems with this perspective is that it divorces or fragments economic activity from the rest of life and has made it so easy for the capitalist to ignore the social and ecological costs of his or her economic activity. When economic activity is reduced to individual self-interest and competition, then it is easy to dump toxins into rivers or use abusive labor practices.

Transaction Position — Rational Planning

The transaction position is based on the assumption that humans can intervene to improve their affairs in a rational manner. Particularly helpful in this intervention process is the scientific method. John Dewey believed that the social sciences had progressed to the point where men could make ''intelligence and ideas the supreme force for the settlement of social issues.'' Pragmatists influenced the growth of social improvement schemes, particularly city planning. For example, Robert Park, a contemporary of Dewey's at the University of Chicago, believed that one could control the physical environment of the city so that the people would experience better physical and mental health. Charles Morris (1986) believes that Dewey and Park were forerunners of the social engineering that pervaded the Kennedy–Johnson years.

> The social-engineering bias was identical in its rationalist premises to the concepts of Lyndon Johnson's Great Society forty years later. Society was like a machine. With enough research, you could understand how the parts fit together — ''model'' it, in latter-day jargon — then by adroitly manipulating the social inputs, you would produce predictable improvements in the outputs: people would be healthier, friendlier, more industrious. (p. 10)

In the early 1960s the social engineering seemed to work. The economy boomed with low inflation and the social programs during the early Johnson years were carried out with great enthusiasm. Social engineering was applied to foreign affairs in the form of the intervention in Vietnam. Here the assumptions of pragmatism and social engineering began to founder. The Vietnamese resistance to American force was much greater than the technocrats had predicted. Both the tactical and moral failure of the Vietnamese adventure contributed greatly to the counter-culture and planted the seeds of present-day transformational perspectives. Paul Warnke, upon leaving the Pentagon in 1969, stated that the problem with the North Vietnamese was that they did not behave like reasonable people. The rationalist model can never fully anticipate how an individual or a group of individuals will act.

Not only did rational planning and intervention break down in Vietnam, it also foundered in economics. Ever since the 1930s governments had tended to rely on Keynesian theory, which used deficit spending to stimulate the economy. However, inflation in the 1970s eroded the Keynesian consensus. Supply side economics replaced belief in government intervention to stimulate the economy. In general, ''New Deal'' liberals became discredited and liberalism searched for alternatives, particularly those associated with new technologies.

Yet the faith in technology holds the same difficulties as the belief in rational planning. Kirkpatrick Sale calls this belief in technology *technofix*. As an example of technofix thinking, Sale (1980) cites former Atomic Energy Commission Chairman Glenn T. Seaborg, who said, "We must pursue the idea, that it is more science, better science, more wisely applied that is going to free us from (our) predicaments . . . and to set the underlying philosophy for a rationale for the future handling of our technological and social development." (p. 35) The technofix solution for anxiety is Valium and for the oil shortage it is coal liquification.

The limitation of technology continues to alarm us, however. In 1986 we had the U. S. shuttle disaster and melt-down at Chernobyl in the Soviet Union to remind us that technology is only as good as the bureaucracies that use it. In short, technology does not operate in a socio-political vacuum. Only when we begin to look at problems in a connected, holistic way can we move beyond the fragmentation of laissez-faire thinking and the naïveté of technofix.

Transformation Position: An Interdependent Perspective

An interdependent perspective regarding social-economic-political thinking starts with the assumption that all human activity is interconnected and thus a change introduced in one area can have effects in other areas. This approach is based on several principles:

1. An ecological sense;
2. Human-scale organizations;
3. Non-Violence; and
4. Androgyny.

An Ecological Sense

An ecological sense starts with the premise that human life is only part of a much larger fabric that includes plants, animals, and the entire biosphere in which we live. We have many examples of how humans both today and in the past have ignored this ecological awareness. One example comes from the Roman Empire, which overharvested the lands around the Mediterranean to feed its large urban populations. The farming techniques led to a run-off of topsoil and eventually the desertification of much of the land, particularly in North Africa. It was the Roman Empire's lack of ecological sense that was mainly responsible for the Sahara Desert.

Today, of course, erosion continues to occur around the world. In the United States, the Army Corps of Engineers reported in 1978 that nearly half of the continental U.S. coastline was suffering from severe erosion with about 21 percent of the coastline classified as "critical." We are often guilty of ecological hubris in that we continue to ignore the ecological context and often suffer as a result. For example, developers continue to build homes on the hills around Los Angeles despite evidence that continued building robs the soil of its absorbent cover. Thus, the soil continues to erode and leads to millions of dollars of damage with high rainfall as homes are destroyed by mudslides. The following letter to the *New York Times* in 1978 expresses ecological hubris very well:

48

To the Editor:

According to all the Judeo-Christian religions, as expressed in the biblical word which they all accept as divinely authoritative, God gave man, made in His image and likeness, dominion over all the earth and its hosts. Then why must we tolerate being subjected to the wild caprices of unstable air masses, including the ultimate obscenity called the tornado, in which a wayward, rapidly rotating air funnel deals death and destruction with impunity to whatever happens to lie in its path?

Why don't the world's leading scientific minds and its political leaders, starting here in this country and possibly operating through the United Nations, give top priority to subjugating the earth's atmosphere, making it totally and abjectly responsive to the well-being and security not of mankind alone but of all life on earth, as well as the solid structures and tools of man's devising?

My blood boils every time I read that a high wind or the pressure gradient in an air mass constituting a tornado kills people, wrecks buildings, tosses cars around like playthings, etc., often as not without the slightest warning. Let us have "weather by the consent of the weathered" and force the elements to respect our wishes! . . . (Cited in Sale, 1980, p. 15)

A few months later the Federal Weather Modification Advisory Board, established under the National Weather Modification Act of 1976, suggested that in twenty years they would be able to control the weather over the country.

How serious are our ecological problems? G. Evelyn Hutchinson (1970) wrote in the *Scientific American* that our biosphere may be able to support life for just a few more decades.

What are examples of an ecological sense? Of course, nature itself provides many examples. Fritjof Capra (1982, p. 281) has described the interconnections in the following manner.

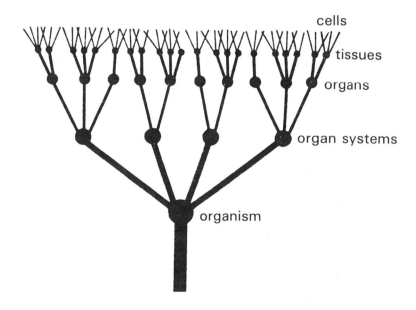

According to Capra (1982), nature is composed of interconnected systems that form multilevelled structures. At each level there are "integrated, self-organizing wholes consisting of smaller parts and at the same time, acting as parts of larger wholes." (p. 280). For example the person is an organism made up of organ systems (for example, the respiratory system), which are composed of organs (the lungs), which are made up of tissue (lung tissue), which in turn are composed of cells. However, each of these levels is a subsystem. Arthur Koestler described such subsystems as a "holon," which has both independent properties of a whole and related properties because it is part of a system. In this context, it is possible to view the universe as a related set of minds — "individual human minds are embedded in the larger minds of social and ecological systems, and these are integrated into the planetary mental system — the mind of Gaia — which in turn must participate in some kind of universal or cosmic mind." (Capra, 1982, p. 292)

Sale (1980) argues that the use of solar energy reflects an ecological sense. First, it does not pollute and is a quiet, odor-free form of energy. It does not use fossil fuels and thus conserves nature's resources. It is also suited to small-scale operations and can be controlled by the people who use it. The sun's energy cannot be monopolized by a few energy companies; for example, in 1979 there were a thousand separate firms in the solar energy business. Solar energy is also very flexible, as a solar unit can be constructed in a matter of days or weeks while a nuclear power plant takes several years or even decades to plan and build. Solar energy is efficient in that very little energy is lost through conversion and transmission. This is in contrast to usual sources of energy used by electrical utilities where 50 to 65 percent of the original energy is lost through conversion and transmission. The technology associated with solar energy is relatively simple and does not require complex delivery systems or large storage capacities. Finally, solar energy is adaptable to any sort of thermodynamic job. Water can be easily heated to be used for hot water, electrical generation, or for even steel manufacturing.

In contrast, nuclear energy requires that uranium reach 2400 degrees and then all the heat has to be drained away to heat a house at 70 degrees, an incredibly inefficient process. Of course, the question rises: Why is solar energy not more widely used? The question of use raises the problem that in industrialized countries there are already large powerful structures (electrical utilities and oil companies) that have a vested interest in the present forms of energy. To expand the use of solar energy one must examine it as a part of the larger process of moving toward what Sale (1980) calls a human-scale society. In short, ecological intervention strategies must be adopted.

As mentioned earlier, the model for an ecological sense comes from nature itself. Nature can be a reminder of the connectedness of all beings, a relationship that Lewis Thomas (1975) acknowledges in his discussion of the bacteria in his body:

> There they are, moving about in my cytoplasm. . . . They are much less closely related to me than to each other and to the free-living bacteria out under the hill. They feel like strangers, but the thought comes that the same creatures, precisely the same, are out there in the cells of seagulls, and whales, and dune grass, and seaweed and hermit crabs, and further inland in the leaves of the beech in my backyard, and in the family of skunks beneath the back fence, and even in that fly on the window. Through them, I am connected: I have close relatives, once removed, all over the place. (p. 86)

Human-Scale Organizations

Kirkpatrick Sale (1980) has written a book entitled *Human Scale* in which he describes how human beings need to live and work in organizations that are reasonable in size. In short "man is the measure" has been the guide for centuries. Sale (1980) claims:

> Was that not the explicitly stated principle of Pericles, of Leonardo, of Jefferson, of Corbusier, and hundreds of others of our most capable planners and thinkers? Indeed, is it not the essential spirit within Jewish mythology, Christian ethics, Anglo-Saxon law, Renaissance humanism, Protestant separatism, merchant capitalism, the French Revolution, the American Republic, Marxism, Darwinism, Freudianism, of so many of the basic currents — though by no means all, of course — of Western history? So in any search for a desirable future, for the ways in which tools, buildings, communities, cities, shops, offices, factories, meeting places, forums, and legislatures should be constructed, I see no reason to go beyond this simple rule: they should all be built to human scale. (p. 37)

Human scale is a term originally associated with architecture where buildings are built that do not dwarf the individual or the surroundings. Human scale means that buildings allow that natural world to coexist with the man-made world. Sale, however, feels that human scale can be applied to economics, health care, education, in fact, most areas of human activity. Sale argues that there are already many examples of human-scale communities, including: the solar-powered community of Davis, California; the Quaker meeting; the worker-controlled industries in Yugoslavia; the communes in Israel; the town meetings in New England communities; the restructuring of many corporations along non-authoritarian lines.

The central values of human scale include individual fulfillment, "community cooperation, harmony with nature, decentralization of power, and self-sufficiency" (p. 46). Sale believes that a number of trends in today's society are supporting the move to human scale. These include the consumer movement, the back-to-nature spirit that prompted a threefold increase of visits to national parks from 1960 to 1978, the so-called "underground economy" which allows people to barter and trade services outside of the standard market place, the co-operative movement — which includes credit unions, health co-ops, food co-ops, and electricity co-ops — and the do-it-yourself movement.

Our modern cities are good examples of environments not built to human scale. In particular, the skyscraper does not let us view the building as a whole but dominates the landscape in almost forbidding manner. One could hypothesize that one of the reasons for the rootlessness of modern city living is the life in the high rise apartment and office buildings. If one lives in a high rise apartment and then works in a high rise office, the only contact with the earth may be the short walk on the concrete sidewalk to the subway. The city inhabitant, then, never feels that he or she is part of an organic environment. Despite some of the problems of suburban living, the two-storey house is a much better example of human-scale building. The average home has windows on all sides where we can see green grass and trees. The doors and doorknobs are built for the human frame and not a race of giants. The fireplace in the home is often the place for the family to gather — a practice that has its roots in the colonial custom of placing the family's prized possessions and furniture around the fireplace. Bloomer and Moore (1977) conclude:

Offices, apartment, and stores are piled together in ways which owe more to filing-cabinet systems or the price of land than to a concern for human existence or experience. In this tangle the American single-family house maintains a curious power over us in spite of its well-publicized inefficiencies of land use and energy consumption. Its power, surely, comes from its being the one piece of the world around us which still speaks directly of our bodies as the center and the measure of that world. (p. 4)

One of the principal examples of human-scale living is the village. Richard Critchfield (1983) makes a strong case for villages being one of the central features of human life for centuries. Sale (1980) claims that anthropological evidence suggests that the oldest human institution is not the family but the village or tribe. The family has usually been a subunit in a somewhat larger community. This larger community — the tribe or village — has been the source of language and culture. There is evidence that once the village or tribe reached over five or six thousand people it became too complex and would self-destruct or readjust (Sale, 1980, pp. 185-87).

Critchfield has lived in villages around the world for a quarter of a century. Although there are some aspects of village life that he does not like (for example, male domination), there are many aspects that represent a form of life that is integrated and organic. For example, in the village the people feel a strong bond to the land. The life of the village is tied closely to the land and the people of the village usually feel a reverence for it. The morale of the villagers is closely related to their work on the land and it is often high when they are harvesting and working hard; it tends to fall during periods of idleness.

Morality in villages is linked with the work on the land and encourages monogamous, divorceless, multi-child marriages. In brief, there is belief in hard work and in a moral code that provides a sense of continuity for the villager. However, the villager tends to be skeptical of formal religion; instead, they have a quite strong personal faith in a God that watches over their personal welfare. In general, the villager lives in a world fused with meaning. Critchfield makes the point that all of the world's great religions come from villages. While western urban civilization has given us nationalism, socialism, communism, capitalism, and democracy, it has never produced a spirituality that guides peoples lives. Critchfield (1983) claims:

> The Western political ideologies of nationalism, socialism, communism, capitalism and democracy have all emerged in cities. No great religion ever has. Abraham was a herdsman, Zoroaster raised cattle, Jesus was a village carpenter's son, Mohammed a shepherd and later a petty trader and Buddha, though a Hindu prince, came from a remote backwater of Nepal. These religions were all formed as little village traditions in revolt against existing city traditions which had somehow failed millions of villagers, just as the Westernization of the great Third World cities so often fails them now. They all emerged in civilizations which, like ours, were in extremis. Prophets come from villages. (p. 234)

It could be argued that there is a rootedness in village life that allows people to be in touch with their Selves. The prophet presents a unified worldview that appeals to our centres.

Critchfield does see a number of changes occurring in villages around the world. Technology is being applied to farming methods, contraception is being widely practised, and the role of women is gradually changing in some villages. In his almost twenty-five years of travel in the villages of the Third World, however, Critchfield has become more concerned about the future of the West. At the conclusion of his book, Critchfield argues for a synthesis of village life with the technological progress of the West:

> The years in the villages have been enough to persuade me that a good many of these people are going to make it and that along the way they'll have lots to tell us. Our lives are not meant to be perpetually fun, self-absorbed Carnavals, reaching for the fast buck and getting zonked out on consumer goodies; that way, when the party's over, you can end up in the kicked-in-the-ribs purgatory of the emergency room. Nor are they meant to be one long back-breaking drudgery over a hoe or a plow.
>
> Certainly, we, with all our technology, wealth and freedom of individual choice, and they, with their closeness to nature and the self-responsibility that comes with living in groups, can come up with something a little better, a way to live that combines the best of our material goods with their simplicity and truth.
>
> We're not all villagers. But our grandfathers were. And so our grandchildren may become. In this book I've made many us-and-them distinctions. But I'll bet you've discovered little about these villagers that you don't recognize. Go to a village and you can't go too far wrong if you assume that everybody is just like you. For in the largest sense, and in those human qualities that really count, on this rather small planet there is only one big us. (p. 338)

Critchfield, like Sale, foresees the change to human-scale organizations in the West.

Human-Scale Schools

Sale also argues for human-scale educational institutions. He refers to studies done by Barker and Gump (1964) on the variable of size and its effect in secondary school settings. Barker and his colleagues spent three years studying thirteen high schools in eastern Kansas. The schools ranged in size from 40 to 2000 students and Barker focussed on how size was related to student participation in athletics, class discussion, and extra-curricular activities. In such activities as music, drama, journalism, and student government, participation was highest in the schools with enrollments between 61 and 150. According to Barker and Gump, the students in the smaller schools felt "more satisfactions relating to the development of competence, to being challenged, to engaging in important actions, to being involved in group activities, and to achieving moral and cultural values."

With regard to classroom activities the bigger school can offer more subjects, but the students in the larger schools participate in fewer classes and variety of classes than the small school students. In the music classes, which were studied in detail, Barker and Gump found that musical education and experience were more widely distributed in the small school.

Other studies support Barker and Gump. Wicker (1969) found that the cognitive complexity of students in smaller high schools (for example, junior classes of twenty to fifty students) was significantly higher than in the larger high schools (for example, junior classes of about 400 students). Similarly, Baird (1969) found in a sample of 21 371 high school students, that high school size has a considerable effect on student achievement, with the smaller schools showing advantages in writing, dramatics, and music. In 1966 James Coleman found that one of the main factors affecting school achievement for students was their sense of control over their own destiny. It could be argued that the small school can contribute to their sense of control.

In reviewing studies that examine different institutions dealing with children the World Health Organization (WHO) concludes that institutions should be small, for example, no larger than a hundred children. According to WHO, when organizations grow above this number, informal discipline based on personal contact is replaced by impersonal, institutional authority.

In general, North American school systems have concentrated on consolidation of programs and moved toward larger schools. For example, in the United States the average size of the elementary school rose from 153 in 1950 to 405 in 1975. At the same time violence and vandalism in schools has skyrocketed. Of course, other factors in society have contributed to school violence, but it could be argued that the increasing size of the school has contributed to the trend of violence.

Larger schools are usually justified on economies of scale; that is, savings arise from joint administration and the use of one plant as opposed to several buildings. However, there are the costs of bussing, the existence of larger bureaucracies associated with larger school systems, and the social costs that can come from closing schools in small communities where the school is often integral to the social life of the town. Another supposed advantage of the larger school is efficiency. However, one study in Vermont (Sher, 1977) indicated that the larger schools were often less efficient because of administrations which are often isolated from the community and the students. The same study indicated that six of the top ten schools in Vermont in percentage of graduates entering college were small (fewer than sixty in the graduating class), and that they were able to produce these results with operating costs on a per pupil basis of $225 less than the large schools.

If human scale is the measure for our institutions, how are we to get there? This brings us to the third principle of an interdependent perspective: non-violent change.

Non-Violent Change

The tenets of non-violence have been articulated by Thoreau, Tolstoy, Gandhi, and King. Non-violent change is based on the principle that one's opponent should not be objectified. Erikson discusses this in *Gandhi's Truth,* which is about the strike at the textile factory in Ahmedabad. Gandhi never reduced his opponent — the mill owners — to objects of hate and condemnation. In Erikson's description, he always left the room in the encounter so that a degree of mutuality might develop between the opponents.

Central to the notion of change here is the respect for the person's individual conscience. Thoreau, in particular, believed that morality should rest on personal conscience. In his famous essay "Resistance to Civil Government," he argues for resistance to unjust laws and governments through non-participation and non-co-operation. Non-violence does not mean passivity. Thoreau calls for non-payment of taxes that support war and slavery. Thoreau also suggests that in an unjust society the appropriate place for the just person may be jail. Of course, this idea was adopted by Gandhi and King in their protests. Richardson (1986) connects this strand in

Thoreau's thinking to Stoicism. Ellery Channing, Thoreau's contemporary, said that Thoreau was a natural stoic.

Stoicism contains many of the principles of holism. The stoic Marcus Aurelius (d. 180; 1964) said: "Always think of the universe as one living organism, with a single substance and a single soul . . . there is a law that governs the course of nature and should govern human actions" (p. 73). Richardson claims that "in contrast to Epicureanism, which held that the universe is made up of atoms and empty space, the Stoics held that God is immanent in all created things, but has no separate existence outside them" (p. 190). The Stoics believed strongly in the individual and personal conscience. Thoreau was able to link his concern for the individual with his love of nature and his ethics. Richardson (1986) concludes:

> Thoreau is probably the greatest spokesman of the last two hundred years for the view that we must turn not to the state, not to a God, and not to society, but to nature for our morality. He stands as the most attractive American example — as Emerson was the great proponent — of the ageless Stoic principle of self-trust, self-reverence, or self-reliance, as it is variously called. Thoreau's life can be thought of as one long uninterrupted attempt to work out the practical concrete meaning of the Stoic idea that the laws ruling nature rule men as well. (p. 191)

Related to the issue of non-violence is reverence for life. It is difficult to injure a living thing if one sees all life as part of a connected whole. How can you injure someone when you see the person as part of yourself?

In contrast to Marxism, change is viewed more organically and connected to one's inner being. The goal in non-violent change is not just to reform society with more appropriate laws and institutions but to seek more fundamental change within the person. So often political revolution has often replaced one form of repression (right-wing dictatorship) with another form (totalitarian communism). One type of élite replaces another. People often try to become "good Marxists" and thus they give up to their own subjectivity; in other words, they adopt a social role rather than listening to the deeper part of themselves. This is also a problem in so-called New Age movements as people try to conform to some ideal (for example, the good Waldorfian).

From a holistic perspective it is important to work from inside-out. Change, then, should be congruent with our centre, not according to some external set of expectations. King and Gandhi were able to reach the deepest part of the person and thus were able to bring about non-exploitative change.

Marxism vs. Holism

Because I have mentioned Marxism several times, and because it is the principal alternative to liberalism, I would like to discuss why ultimately it is inadequate as a basis for personal and social growth.

First, it should be recognized that Marxism in its various forms is the dominant alternative ideology in our universities, particularly in sociology departments. Marxism has a long intellectual history and many of the brightest minds, such as Michael Apple and Henry Giroux, argue its merits very persuasively.

Second it appeals to our sense of guilt. Since Marxism is a philosophy which purports to end social and economic oppression, when we subscribe to its tenets we may feel less guilty about our affluence when compared to Third World peoples. It provides an activist philosophy that promises to set things right.

Finally, it can be viewed as a religion or a way of life. Mark Satin (1978) says:

> . . . Marxism seems to me and to many other observers to be a kind of substitute religion. Consider the use of religious language in Marxism (e.g., Marx and Engels first considered calling the Communist Manifesto the Communist Catechism). Consider the use of the works of Marx and Engels to settle arguments and justify policies — just like some devout people use the Bible or the Koran. Henry Mayo says that Marxism "may be regarded as a revelation, a gospel of deliverance to the poor" — and that the proletariat may be regarded as "a kind of Chosen people, who alone will possess the New Jerusalem." After the revolution will come the Great Judgment — the dictatorship of the proletariat — to separate the proletarian sheep from the bourgeois goats. Beyond the struggle lies — the millennium. Eden before the Fall bears a striking resemblance to the stage of primitive communism. In both monolithic religion and Marxism, there is the same belief in inevitability, the same belief in ultimate victory — guaranteed by the "eternal laws: of history and the universe." And there is the same claim to universally valid truths. (pp. 270-71)

Marx took the work of Hegel, namely the dialectic, and applied it to economic change. However, Marx dismissed the idealism of Hegel and argued that the economic system of a society is the central feature. He focussed primarily on economic determinism and argued that eventually capitalism will destroy itself and be replaced by a dictatorship of the proletariat and then a classless society. The change will be brought about through class conflict as the bourgeoisie who own the capital become very few in number in contrast to the large numbers of the proletariat. The proletariat, many of them unemployed, eventually unite and easily take over power from the bourgeoisie. This view of change is called scientific socialism and centres on economic materialism, determinism, and class conflict.

One of the problems with Marxism is the objectification of the person. There is simply no recognition of the inner life of the individual and if there is, it is simply reduced to economic explanations. What we have in Marxism are faceless individuals whose identity is based on their class. More than that, the classes are divided into the good guys (proletariat) and the bad guys (bourgeoisie) and there is no compassion for the bad guys. Finally, Marxism is materialist and does not acknowledge the spiritual side of human nature. There is no room for awe or mystery in Marxism. No wonder the "realistic" art of communist countries is so stifling.

As I mentioned earlier, it is possible for holism to become objectified as people attempt to conform to the Aquarian conspiracy or another New Age ideal, but this is against the spirit of holism, which focusses on connectedness, compassion, and reaching our inner Self. Ultimately, there is not one vision of society proposed by holism but alternatives. More importantly, how we achieve the goal of a more human-scale society is as important as the goal itself. If we are forced to manipulate or treat people as objects then this ultimately will corrupt any goal we achieve.

Androgyny

As we contact our centre, we become more whole. This means that we let go of roles for which we have been conditioned; for example, sexual roles. Androgyny means that we no longer think of ourselves as exclusively masculine or feminine; instead we can begin to see ourselves as whole people comprised of opposites or polarities within us. This does not mean that men, for example, must necessarily become more sensitive or emotional, it only means that we can awaken to the polarities within us. Feminine and masculine can be viewed in relation to polarities such as:

Ying	Yang
intuitive	rational
holistic	analytic
responsive	initiating
nurturing	achieving
contracting	expanding

From our centre we can open to and work these polarities rather than get caught in one set of qualities. If we get caught up in one polarity, we close ourselves off to part of our own being. Research indicates that people who are able to integrate these polarities can more readily comprehend ambiguous information and deal with the co-existence of incongruous qualities within one person (Tripodi and Bieri, 1966; Halverson, 1970) and can more easily change (Pelia, Crockett and Gonyea, 1970). Several psychologists, including Erikson, Jung, Singer, and Maslow, have also claimed that the ability to accept and then integrate the different parts of oneself is a sign of psychological growth. For example, Maslow (1942) found that self-actualizing men and women are similar in their transcendence of traditional male–female stereotypes.

Despite this acceptance of polarities by certain psychologists, in the West we have tended to accept one set of qualities (masculine-yang) as desirable and the other set (feminine-ying) as less desirable. In contrast, the Eastern approach sees the polarities as related to one another and as part of a larger whole. Either/or conceptualization is problematic in that it forces us to accept a limited identity. According to Olds (1981), working with both polarities can move us to higher levels of consciousness:

> Often the mode of liberation comes precisely through the heightening of tension between two incompatible modes of thought or concepts. The leverage point for new alternatives of thought or action lies in the posing of paradox and the simultaneous existence of two incompatible thoughts or commands. This is the method of Zen (Suzuki, 1964) and of the Yaqui sorcerer in Castaneda's (1968, 1971) writings who helps him break through the interpretive webs he confuses with reality by flowing back and forth between discrepant, alternative world views and learning to "see." Thus wholeness, synthesis, and the transcending of polarity seem to characterize the human ideal in philosophic speculation as well as in psychological health. (p. 19)

Androgyny is another metaphor for wholeness. The word is derived from the Greek andros (man) and gyne (woman). June Singer (1976), working from a Jungian framework, has been one of the main proponents of androgyny as a metaphor for wholeness; she sees it as rediscovered archetype and inner guide. It is also possible to see androgyny as a cultural and social norm rather than a purely psychological term. For example, Bem (1972, 1974, 1975b) has concentrated on androgyny as a social norm which could promote a less exploitive society. From this perspective androgyny is not limited to the struggle for equal rights for women. Its broader aim is to balance our Western emphasis on technology, competitiveness, individualism, and logical thinking, with the feminine values of nurturing co-operation, relatedness, and love. Olds sees the restoration of feminine values as a vehicle for a broad cultural synthesis.

> The ultimate form of revolution, in fact, might be a kind of revolution in consciousness and spirituality involving the transcendence of duality and dichotomous thinking in all spheres, unleashing tremendous cultural crossbreeding, synthesis, and integration. The revaluation of the feminine mode of consciousness as part of an androgynous goal augurs well for both scientific renewal and spiritual evolution, broadening the parameters of each pursuit and enlarging the scope of our inquiry. (p. 245)

There is a danger, however, of being too rigid in our ideal of androgyny. Perhaps it is more helpful to view it as a useful metaphor. If we define too limited an ideal, then people will feel a need to conform to this ideal and feel guilty if they don't. Thus the woman who stresses caring as a principle for her life might feel uneasy if she is not working, and the man who works and cannot be at home as much as he would like can become guilty about not fulfilling his role at home. Again we need to turn to our centre as a guide in working with inner polarities.

Summary

The social context for the holistic curriculum consists of an environment where wholeness is valued and in which people can interact in human-scale communities. The following chart summarizes the characteristics of social contexts associated with each of the three positions.

Transmission	Transaction	Transformation
laissez-faire	rational planning	economic activity linked to social/ecological awareness
conservative	liberal	transcending traditional polarities
competition	regulated competition	co-operation/regulated competition
big business tends to dominate market place	big business and big government dominate	human-scale economies
decisions based on profit/loss	centralized decision-making often by bureaucracy	decentralized decision-making that includes social and ecological costs

nature and economic activity viewed as separate	nature and economic activity linked through rational planning	nature and economic activity seen as inter-connected
hard data	quantative data used (for example, mathematical models)	emphasis on quality, hard and soft data integrated
human needs deter-mined by market place/advertising	needs influencing by rational planning	needs viewed organically; appropriate consumption
individual roles linked to market (for ex-ample, specialization)	roles linked to liberal, democratic theory (for example, inalienable rights)	roles linked to fulfill-ment-connection to community
narrow sex roles	flexible roles linked to equal rights legislation	androgyny/transcending sex roles
change determined by market fluctuations	rational/planned change	non-violent change responding to inner needs
short-term view	longer-term view linked to planning	evolutionary, organic view of change
top down organizations	democratic organizations; rational consensus	consensus includes aware-ness of spiritual and emotional needs

References

Aurelius, Marcus. *Meditations.* New York: Penguin, 1964.

Baird, L. ''Big School, Small School: A Critical Examination of the Hypothesis,'' *Journal of Educational Psychology* 60, 4(1) (August 1969), 253-60.

Barker, R. B., and Gump, P. V. *Big School, Small School.* Palo Alto, California: Stanford University Press, 1964.

Bem, S. L. ''Psychology Looks at Sex Roles: Where Have All the Androgynous People Gone?'' Unpublished Paper Presented at UCLA Symposium on Women, 1972.

Bem, S. L. ''The Measurement of Psychological Androgyny.'' *Journal of Consulting and Clinical Psychology* 42 (1974), 155-62.

Bieri, J. ''Cognitive-Simplicity as a Personality Variable in Cognitive and Preferential Behavior.'' In *Functions of Varied Experience,* edited by D. W. Fiske and S. R. Maddi. Homewood, Illinois: Dorsey Press, 1961.

Bloomer, K. C., and Moore, C. W. *Body, Memory and Architecture.* New Haven, Connecti-cut: Yale University Press, 1977.

Delia, J. G.; Crockett, W. H.; and Gonyea, A. H. "Cognitive Complexity and the Effects of Schemas on the Learning of Social Structures." Proceedings of the Annual Convention of the American Psychological Association 5 (1970), 373-74.

Capra, Fritjof. *The Turning Point.* New York: Simon and Schuster, 1982.

Critchfield, Richard. *Villages.* Garden City, New York: Anchor Press/Doubleday, 1983.

Erikson, Erik. *Gandhi's Truth.* New York: W. W. Norton, 1969.

Friedman, M., and Friedman, R. *Free to Choose.* San Diego, California: Harcourt Brace Jovanovich, 1980.

Halverson, C. F. "Interpersonal Perception: Cognitive Complexity and Trait Implication." *Journal of Consulting and Clinical Psychology* 34 (1970), 86-90.

Heilbroner, R. L. *The Worldly Philosophers.* New York: Touchstone Books, 1980.

Hutchinson, G. E. "The Biosphere." *Scientific American,* vol. 223(3) (September 1970), pp. 44-53.

Maslow, A. H. "Self Esteem (Dominance Feeling) and Sexuality in Women." *Journal of Social Psychology,* 16 (1942), 259-94.

Morris, C. R. *A Time of Passion: America 1960-80.* New York: Penguin Books, 1986.

Olds, L. E. *Fully Human.* Englewood Cliffs, N.J.: Prentice Hall, 1981.

Richardson, R. D. *Henry David Thoreau: A Life of the Mind.* Berkeley, California: University of California Press, 1986.

Sale, K. *Human Scale.* New York: Perigee Books, 1980.

Satin, M. *New Age Politics.* New York: Delta, 1978.

Sher, J. O. *Education in Rural America.* Boulder, Colo: Westview Press, 1977.

Singer, J. *Androgyny: Toward a New Theory of Sexuality.* Garden City, New York: Anchor Press/Doubleday, 1976.

Thomas, L. *The Lives of a Cell.* New York: Bantam, 1975.

Tripoldi, T., and Bieri, J. "Cognitive Complexity, Perceived Conflict, and Certainty." *Journal of Personality,* 34 (1966) 144-53.

Wicker, A. "Cognitive Complexity, School Size, and Participation in School Behavior Settings: A Test of the Frequency of Interaction Hypothesis." *Journal of Educational Psychology* 60, 3 (June 1969), 200-203.

Part II

Holistic Curriculum: Practice

4

Holistic Curriculum: Historical Background

The holistic curriculum is not new. Educators and philosophers have articulated its principles and used it for centuries. However, each age has had to redefine the holistic curriculum in its own terms. The major problem confronting holistic educators has been integrating the two strands.

One strand has concentrated on personal growth. Within this strand there has been a further division between psychological growth (humanistic educators) and those individuals who focus on spiritual growth (transpersonal educators). Of course, the line between these substrands is not always clear, as the transpersonal educators usually include psychological development as a component of spiritual growth.

The other strand has focussed on social change. From this position educators have developed programs that encourage student involvement in the community. This involvement can take the form of service to the community or social action. The latter is somewhat more radical as the student tries to effect some change or improvement in the life of the community.

The holistic curriculum has been most effective when these strands have been integrated as in the Modern School of New York and Stelton.

Socrates and Plato

Socrates' "know thyself" can be viewed as one of the first guidelines for holistic education. Socrates, with his relentless questioning, forced the individual to examine his or her own assumptions. Self-examination is based, in part, on the premise that all knowledge lies within and that we can discover it by contemplation. Socrates and Plato believed that the soul existed before birth and that by being put in a physical body it had forgotten its true identity. This is called the "Doctrine of Reminiscence" (Ozman and Carver, 1981, p. 5). Socrates, then, acted as a midwife to draw our ideas that lay within the person. Plato, in the *Meno* dialogue, describes how Socrates extracts the Pythagorean theorem from a slave boy through questioning.

One of the methods that Socrates used and Plato recommended was the dialectic where the person intensely examines both sides of an issue so that a synthesis can occur. Sometimes referred to as Socratic dialogue, the dialectic requires skillful questioning or otherwise it can merely encourage the person to entrench his or her thinking.

Plato described his approach to education in *The Republic*. He suggested a comprehensive educational system run by the state which would develop people to their full potential. Education for Plato should teach the person to see beyond the impermanence of the material world and intuit the "real world" of ideas. Plato's allegory of the cave could also be seen as a metaphor for education. In this allegory prisoners are in darkness and in chains and they see only shadows on the walls of the cave. However, one of the prisoners walks up a steep slope and eventually into the sunlight. He realizes that he has been living in a world of illusion and returns to the cave to explain to his fellow prisoners his discovery. However, explaining his discovery to the prisoners involves risk, because they may not believe that they are living in a world of shadows. Plato felt that the philosopher-teacher should take the risk and share his or her knowledge with others. Thus, the teacher cannot remain in contemplation but must enter into the world and engage in dialogue with others.

Augustine

Augustine, who lived in the period of the late Roman Empire, was influenced by Plato and developed an intuitive approach to education. For Augustine, however, the dialectic was basically a method for spiritual development. There are a number of written dialogues between Augustine and his illegitimate son, Adeodatus, that focus on the search for God.

Augustine believed that the ultimate good lay within the individual and that education must lead the person within to discover this truth. He encouraged meditation to bring out the truth that lay within the soul. Augustine influenced the monastic tradition and religious education with his emphasis on intuition and meditation. Intuition, meditation, and visualization are discussed later in the book (chapters 5 and 9).

Rousseau

Perhaps the most important historical figure in relation to the humanist strand in holistic education is Rousseau. His book *Emile* was published in 1762, and in it he described his approach to education. Rousseau advocated a natural approach to child-rearing, as he believed the natural soul of the child was good and must be protected from civilization. He said: "From the outset raise a wall round your child's soul" or it will be overcome by "the crushing force of social conventions" (1955, p. 6). This romantic view of the child has continued to inspire humanistic and alternative school educators.

In *Emile*, Rousseau describes four stages of development — infancy, childhood, youth, and adulthood. These stages are described in four parts of the book, and in the last part Rousseau describes the education of Sophy. At the heart of his approach is negative education. Rousseau stated:

> Nature provides for the child's growth in her own way and this should never be thwarted. Do not make him sit still when he wants to run about, nor run when

he wants to be quiet. If we did not spoil our children's wills by our blunders their desires would be free from caprice (p. 50) . . . Give him no orders at all, absolutely none (p. 55) . . . Give your scholar no verbal lessons, he should be taught by experience alone; never make him say, "Forgive me",. for he does not know how to do you wrong. Wholly unmoral in his actions, he can do nothing morally wrong, and he deserves neither punishment nor reproof (p. 56). . . There the education of the earliest years should be merely negative. It consists, not in teaching virtue or truth, but in preserving the heart from vice and from the spirit of error.

For Rousseau, then, the child should be allowed to explore the world and make his or her own discoveries.

Of course, it is impossible to devise an education that is totally negative and unsupervised, and there thus exists an inherent contradiction within Rousseau's work and that of most romantic educators such as A. S. Neill. At one point Rousseau says, "Take the opposite course with your pupil; let him always think he is master while you are really master. . . . No doubt he ought only do what he wants but he ought to want to do nothing but what you want him to do" (pp. 84-85). Here Rousseau describes the teacher as manipulator as he devises situations to seduce the child into learning. For example, Rousseau describes a complicated situation with a conjurer at a country fair who teaches Emile about magnets. Emile learns about measuring distance without instruments by playing games in the dark. Negative education, then, is not so easily practised and raises fundamental questions about the role of the teacher.

Pestalozzi and Froebel

Johann Heinrich Pestalozzi, the Swiss educator, was influenced by Rousseau, Locke, and Comenius, and thus his work shows both transactional and transformational influences. He also differs from Rousseau in that he taught most of his life and attempted to put his beliefs into practice. He cared about poor children and devoted much of his life to their education. Morf, in de Guimps (1889), summarizes the major principles of Pestalozzi's approach to education:

1. Intuition is the basis of instruction.
2. Language should be linked with intuition.
3. The time for learning is not the time for judgment and criticism.
4. In every branch, teaching should begin with the simplest elements and proceed gradually according to the development of the child, that is, in psychologically connected order.
5. Sufficient time should be devoted to each point of the teaching in order to ensure the complete mastery of it by the pupil.
6. Teaching should aim at development and not dogmatic exposition.
7. The educator should respect the individuality of the pupil.
8. The chief end of elementary teaching is not to impart knowledge and talent to the learner, but to develop and increase the powers of his intelligence.
9. Power must be linked to knowledge; and skill to learning.
10. The relations between the master and the pupil, especially as to discipline, should be based upon and ruled by love.
11. Instruction should be subordinated to the higher aim of education. (pp. 154-55)

Principles 7 and 10 reflect the Rousseauian influence. Many educational historians (Bayles and Hood, 1966) have argued that the real genius of Pestalozzi was his empathy for children and his ability to adjust his instructional methods to the unique needs of each student. John Ramsauer, one of Pestalozzi's students, describes the informality of his classroom technique:

> There was no regular school plan nor order of lessons; and Pestalozzi did not limit himself to any fixed time, but often went on with the same subject for two or three hours. We numbered about sixty boys and girls from eight to fifteen years of age; our lessons lasted from eight o'clock in the morning till eleven; and in the afternoon from two o'clock till four, and the teaching was limited to drawing, arithmetic and exercises in language.

> There was neither reading nor writing; the pupils had no textbooks nor copy books and they learned nothing by heart. We had neither drawing models nor directions but slates only and red chalk, and whilst Pestalozzi made us repeat sentences about natural history as language exercises, we could draw whatever we liked; some drew little men and women; others houses; others again traced lines and arabesques according to their fancy. Pestalozzi never looked at what we drew or rather scribbled; but by the cuffs and elbows of our coats one could see that the scholars had made use of the red chalk. As for arithmetic we had between every two scholars a little frame divided into squares in which were points that we could count, add, multiply, subtract, and divide. (Ramsauer, in de Guimps, 1889, pp. 104-105)

Froebel was influenced by both Rousseau and Pestalozzi; however, he was more mystical in his conception of education and is quoted in the first chapter of this book. Froebel developed the kindergarten and saw play as an important factor in the young child's development. He said, "play is the first means of development of the human mind, its first effort to make acquaintance with the outward world, to collect original experiences from things and facts, and to exercise the powers of body and mind. The child indeed recognizes no purpose in it, and knows nothing, in the beginning, of any end which is to be reached when it imitates the play it sees around it, but it expresses its own nature, and that is human nature in its playful activity" (quoted in Marenholz-Bulow, 1895, p. 67).

Froebel, like Rousseau, believed in the inherent goodness of the child. He (1887) claimed: ". . . a suppressed or perverted good quality — a good tendency, only repressed, misunderstood, or misguided — lies originally at the bottom of every shortcoming in man" (p. 121). The natural play of the child, then, allows this goodness to unfold.

Leo Tolstoy

Tolstoy, like Froebel and Pestalozzi, was influenced by Rousseau. He felt that children, and peasant children in particular, should be left untouched so that their goodness could unfold. Tolstoy was very critical of school:

> School justly presents itself to the child's mind as an establishment where he is taught that which nobody understands; where he is generally compelled to speak

not in his native patois, Mundart, but a foreign language; where the teacher for the greater part sees in his pupils, his natural enemies, who, out of their own malice and that of their parents, do not wish to learn that which he has learned; and where the pupils, on their side, look upon their teacher as their enemy . . . (Weiner 1967, p. 12)

To provide an alternative Tolstoy established his own school on his Russian estate at Yasnaya Polyana, and here he taught the peasants according to his own theories. He let the children decide whether they would attend the lessons or not. If they did attend, he had them write stories based on their own experience. Troyat (1980) has given us the flavor of Tolstoy's school:

At eight in the morning, a child rang the bell. Half an hour later, "through fog, rain, or the slanting rays of the autumn sun," the black silhouettes of little muzhiks appeared by twos and threes, swinging their empty arms. As in the previous years, they brought no books or notebooks with them — nothing at all, save the desire to learn. The classrooms were painted pink and blue. In one, mineral samples, butterflies, dried plants and physics apparatus lined the shelves. But no books. Why books? The pupils came to the classroom as though it were home; they sat where they liked, on the floor, on the windowledge, on a chair or the corner of a table, they listened or did not listen to what the teacher was saying, drew near when he said something that interested them, left the room when work or play called them elsewhere — but were silenced by their fellow pupils at the slightest sound. Self-imposed discipline. The lessons — if these casual chats between an adult and some children could be called that — went on from eight-thirty to noon and from three to six in the afternoon, and covered every conceivable subject from grammar to carpentry, by way of religious history, singing, geography, gymnastics, drawing and composition. Those who live too far away to go home at night slept in the school. In the summer they sat around their teacher outdoors in the grass. Once a week they all went to study plants in the forest. (p. 227).

A. S. Neill

Perhaps the most famous proponent of humanistic education in this century was A. S. Neill. Neill founded an alternative school in Germany in 1921 which was later moved to England to become the famous Summerhill school. Like Rousseau, Pestalozzi, and Froebel, Neill disliked moralizing or instilling guilt in children.

At Summerhill, children had the choice of going to class or staying away. Teachers tended to run their classes very informally. Croall (1983) comments that Neill "took virtually no interest in teaching methods, and gave no sort of guidance to his teachers as to what they should be doing" (p. 206). Neill was primarily concerned with the emotional life of the child. Parents often sent problem children to Summerhill and Neill excelled in responding to their needs. Because they were not forced to learn and because of Neill's caring presence these children often overcame their difficulties to become healthy individuals. Croall (1983), in his biography of Neill, comments:

Neill's greatest achievement, however, undoubtedly lay in his ability as 'a curer of souls'. A considerable number of adults now leading ordinary unexceptionable lives, owe the fact that they do so to Neill. He himself in later life liked to argue that it was the environment of freedom rather than his individual work with problem children that was responsible for so many startling 'cures'. Many former Summerhill pupils thought otherwise as did several of the adults who worked alongside Neill over the years. To them, it was Neill's humanity and understanding which produced the results. As one former problem child said, looking back over his time at Summerhill: 'I feel almost certain that, had it not been for Neill, I would have ended up in a mental hospital long ago.' (p. 407)

Neil compared his approach to education with Bertrand Russell who had established Beacon Hill school in 1927. Once he commented to Russell that if a child were with them, Russell would want the child to tell him about the stars while Neill would prefer to leave the child with his own thoughts. Croall (1983) concludes that "while Neill aims to release the emotions, Russell wants to train the mind" (p. 159). Neill believed that if "the emotions were free, the intellect will look after itself." (Neill, cited in Croall, 1983, p. 219.)

Neill was the benign authority at Summerhill. Although students did have a great deal of freedom, Neill drew limits in some areas such as the health and safety of the children and the hiring and firing of teaching staff. For example, he made rules about where the children could climb.

One of the central features of the school was the meeting where each person had one vote, including Neill. Here his influence was more subtle. Croall (1983) comments:

> Nona Simon, who came to Summerhill at the age of 4, and was virtually brought up by the Neills, recalls: 'Most little kids would only vote with the majority, and you'd get just as much hero worship of the older children as of Neill. But he would affect the voting — he was an authority without having to say too much.' Branwen Williams takes a similar view: 'Though he would say that we ran the school, that he had no more say at the meetings than anyone else, I think in practice we still looked to him for a lead — certainly when we were very little. We used to outvote him occasionally, just to prove that his theories were right; but I think we were a little uneasy about it. So there was a subtle kind of guidance.' Cynthia Allen reinforces this idea: 'His very withdrawal from a conflict, his departure to his workshop or desk, made an impact,' she remembers. (p. 181)

Neill, like Rousseau and other romantics, was faced with the dilemma of where and how to intervene in the children's life.

Neill's influence beyond the school was immense. By 1969 his book *Summerhill* was selling at a rate of more than 200 000 copies a year. This book was a bible to many free school educators in the 1960s and 1970s as they attempted to set up their own versions of Summerhill. According to Graubard (1972), the number of free schools reached approximately five hundred by 1972. Graubard claims that these schools did away with "all of the public school apparatus of imposed disciplines and punishments, lock-step gradings and time-period divisions, homework, frequent tests and grades and report cards, rigid graded curriculum, standardized classrooms, dominated and commanded by one teacher with 25 to 35 students under his or her power" (p. 40). Unfortunately, these schools did not have Neill as their head. Neill's intuitive genius with children was at the heart of Summerhill's success and could never be replaced in the free schools. Humanistic theory dating back to Rousseau has never been strong and has left zealous educators grouping for strategies to deal with kids.

Open Education Movement

Most of the free schools sprang up outside of the public school system. However, many public school educators sought their own form of humanistic education. Public school systems implemented open education and various forms of affective education. Charles Silberman's book *Crisis in the Classroom* (1970) put open education into the limelight in the United States, while in Ontario the Hall–Dennis report did the same. Open education was an attempt to implement a more child-centred approach in schools through a variety of techniques such as interest centres, classrooms without walls, team teaching, individual instruction, and in providing more choices for learners. Affective education employed various strategies such as values clarification, simulation games, and role-playing to enhance the emotional development of the student.

Ravitch (1983) claims the open education movement failed:

> The open education movement . . . did not survive as a movement because, lacking a definition, it became identified with ideas and practices of its extremely child-centered advocates, those who zealously opposed whatever was traditional in the structure, content, or methods of the classroom. Their ideological tenets stressed the freedom of the child, the passivity of the teacher, equality between teacher and child, the virtues of play and unstructured activity, and distrust of virtues of play and unstructured activity, and distrust of extrinsic motivation. Open classroom teachers who expected their methods to work as the ideology said it would were in for a rude awakening. Nothing prepared them for criticism from parents and other teachers about the noisiness of their classrooms and the neglect of ''basics''. They were taken aback when children demanded that teachers take a more active role or asked to learn from a textbook; they did not know how to deal with discipline problems because they were not suppose to have any. (pp. 254-55)

Open education may have failed in bringing about many of the changes that it intended; however, I believe that his judgment is too harsh and too limited. Open education and affective education did effect a basic concern for treating students with more respect. Now teachers more fully recognize the importance of student self-concept as vital to learning and development. In a more legalistic sense, there is a much stronger recognition of the limits of the teacher's arbitrary authority in dealing with students.

Social Change Education

Social change educators believe that society needs changes, often of a radical nature, and the schools have an important role to play in bringing about the change. It is possible to view Plato's *Republic* as one of the first social change documents to outline the importance of education in its vision of a new society.

Karl Marx believed that education had been used by the capitalists to keep the status quo and to maintain their economic interests. Marxists have claimed that the hidden curriculum of the school reinforces passivity so that workers will accept their role on the assembly line. Textbooks avoid controversial issues and help in the development of the "good citizen" who does what he or she is told. However, Marx also saw that education has a potential for bringing about fundamental change by making people more conscious of their exploitation and raising their social consciousness.

In this century Francisco Ferrer, George Counts, and Theodore Brameld have argued for social change or reconstruction.

Francisco Ferrer

In 1901 Ferrer began the Escuela Moderna for the workers' children of Barcelona, Spain. Ferrer developed an approach called "Rational Education" where the teachers develop the children's critical faculties through inquiry and scientific investigation. Ferrer stated:

> The distinction between justice and injustice is perhaps the first moral distinction which a child can and does grasp and it would be ridiculous to pretend it lies outside the proper sphere of education. Our intrinsic plea that it is not fair to prejudice the mind of a child on subjects he cannot fully understand is nothing but a fallacy of bourgeois self defence. (Archer 1911, p. 48)

Ferrer, unlike Rousseau or Tolstoy, was not content to leave children to their own devices. Instead, he felt that they should be immersed in social issues so that they can develop a critical awareness of social forces. Ferrer suggested that critical literature can help raise the child's consciousness.

> It penetrates to their intelligence and implants in them a rooted conviction of the possibility of a new order of things in which peace and happiness shall reign supreme, very unlike our present condition of social injustice, strife and unhappiness. (Archer 1911, p. 40)

Ferrer particularly liked *The Adventures of Nono* by Jean Grave which builds revolutionary ideas into a fantasy tale. In this tale a ten-year-old boy goes through a series of adventures in places such as "Autonomy" and "Solidarity" and meets people such as "The Capitalist," and "The Workers." When Nono receives a gift from his parents, Grave draws the following point: "not an expensive one, of course, for the parents of Nono were working people, and the rich people squander money on frivolities to such a degree that scarcely anything is left over for the working people to buy their children what they require" (Archer 1911, p. 40).

Ferrer encouraged parents to participate in his school. He also edited a magazine that focussed on syndicalism and contained articles on radical education. Ferrer's work had a strong impact on radical schools in France and Italy and eventually influenced the Modern School in New York, which is discussed at the end of this chapter.

George S. Counts

Counts knew John Dewey and was influenced by Dewey's social activist side. Counts was most famous for his book *Dare the Schools Build a New Social Order?*, which was published in 1932. Counts was horrified by the depression and unemployment. He went to Russia in 1930 and felt the United States should deal more constructively with the problems that faced it. Counts was critical of progressive education, which he felt attempted to avoid controversy under the guise of value neutrality. Counts (1932) claimed:

> If Progressive Education is to be genuinely progressive, it must emancipate itself from the influence of this class, face squarely and courageously every social issue, come to grips with life in all of its stark reality, establish an organic relation with the community, develop a realistic and comprehensive theory of welfare, fashion a compelling and challenging vision of human destiny, and become less frightened than it is today at the bogies of imposition and indoctrination (pp. 9-10).

Critics said that Counts was a communist sympathizer and his call for fundamental change was not accepted by mainstream educators. However, his plea for teachers to become involved in social change continues to prod the consciences of educators.

Theodore Brameld

Brameld is known for developing social reconstructionism into a fully articulated philosophy. Brameld is critical of nationalistic biases and has called for international governments that reflect his desire for world unity. Brameld's work has influenced those who have tried to build a universal or world curriculum.

Brameld argues that we must employ a variety of forces to bring about significant change:

> Socrates said twenty-five hundred years ago, "Know thyself." Marx might have said, "If thou art to know thyself, become conscious of thy class relationships." Freud might have said, "To know thyself, examine thy inner emotional forces." The reconstructionist wishes to transform education into a powerful means for social change toward world civilization. But to accomplish this we must learn how to estimate and direct our energies on all levels of personal and cultural nature. The means are ultimately rational, to be sure, but only if and when they succeed in recognizing the power of the unrational.

> But let me say now that the reconstructionist point of view means fundamental alteration in the curriculum of the schools all the way from kindergarten up through the high schools, the colleges and adult education. The processes of learning and teaching will also be radically altered. Finally, the control of education, including its administration and policy-making, will have to be changed. Thus, the curriculum, the teacher-learning process, and the control of education will all undergo transformation. This, again, is what is implied by a democratically radical philosophy. A philosophy which endorses minor, patchwork changes cannot achieve the required goals. Only a far-reaching, reconstructive approach to education as both ends and means will serve an age such as ours. (p. 40)

Has Brameld's ideal of synthesizing humanistic and social change forces ever been realized? One must answer, rarely. From a historical perspective Florence Tager (1986) claims that The Modern School of New York and Stelton was a synthesis of humanistic and political consciousness.

The Modern School of New York and Stelton, 1911–15

This school was founded on the ideals of Tolstoy and Francisco Ferrer. Ferrer was executed in 1910 and this provided the impetus to found a Ferrer Association in New

York. The Association founded the Ferrer Center, The Modern School, and a journal, *The Modern School*. The Association consisted of workers, socialists, anarchists, and libertarians. Some of the more militant leaders included Emma Goldman and Alexander Berman. The goals of the Association included:

1. To create an education centre for radical thought that would provide evening classes and a reading room consisting of radical literature not available elsewhere in the community.
2. To continue the protests of Ferrer's execution.
3. To found a day school for children along the lines of the Modern School of Spain.
4. To aid all movements for liberation.
   (Kelly, 1913, p. 57)

The school opened in 1911 and the founders believed that libertarian and socialist principles could be combined. The school was based on the belief that children "raised in freedom would refuse oppressive working conditions and become political revolutionaries" (Tager, p. 401). The Modern School was housed in the same building as the Association and contained portraits of Ferrer, Tolstoy, Whitman, Ibsen, and William Morris. Sometimes the children would go to the office where the radical magazine *Mother Earth* was being published. Initially, the pedagogy was Tolstoyean, according to Tager (1986):

> The classroom methodology was libertarian in the Tolstoyean sense. Children arrived at the school when they wished and worked and played at their own pace on the subjects that interested them. The curriculum was often defined by the children themselves. A typical day at the Modern School was described by Will Durant, the teacher at the school in the winter of 1912-1913. According to Durant, the children arrived at different times. When he arrived the children ran to tackle him and continued their friskiness for the next half hour. Then some children studied and worked while others continued rough-housing. Those that were ready for work went into the quiet room where they did lessons in reading and mathematics or did encyclopedia work. The eight older children were given lessons everyday while the younger children received their individual instruction approximately every other day. When the weather permitted, the children would have a picnic lunch in the park and spend the afternoon outside playing and telling stories. (p. 402)

Tager points out there were inevitable conflicts about the philosophy of the school between the political radicals and the libertarians. Although Ferrer remained the guiding image of the school, the day-to-day life in the school was more Tolstoyean. However, the Ferrer Center, which attracted political radicals, influenced the children and the school in a more informal way. Thus, a synthesis of the revolutionary and libertarian strands was effected. One student said, "As much as the Day School meant to me, the center meant more . . . That's where things were happening! I got to know people from all parts of the world and all parts of the radical spectrum" (p. 404).

Members of the Ferrer Association taught at the school and children attended adult classes which were held at the centre. This was also the period of political activity with strikes and demonstrations occurring frequently in New York. This overall climate also had an impact on the school.

Some parents expressed concern about the relaxed curriculum and atmosphere of the school and as a result more academic subjects were added with a stress on history. Classroom activity became less individualistic and more group-oriented. Students contributed to a children's magazine and the decoration of the classroom (Tager, p. 407). Eventually the school moved to Stelton, New Jersey, where under the leadership of Alex and Elizabeth Ferm the school again adopted a more Tolstoyean stance. In general, it was during the New York years that a real synthesis of romantic and political education took place.

There are present-day examples of how humanism and social consciousness can be integrated. A few of the examples include Waldorf Education, Social Literacy Training, and Confluent Education, which are discussed in the following chapters.

References

Archer, William. *The Life, Trial, and Death of Francisco Ferrer.* London: Chapman and Hall, 1911.

Bayles, Ernest E., and Hood, Bruce L. *Growth of American Educational Thought and Practice.* New York: Harper and Row, 1966.

Brameld, Theodore. *Education as Power.* New York: Holt, Rinehart and Winston, Inc., 1965.

Counts, George. *Dare the Schools Build a New Social Order?* New York: Day, 1932.

Croall, Jonathan. *Neill of Summerhill: The Permanent Rebel.* London: Routledge and Kegan Paul, 1983.

De Guimps, R. *Pestalozzi: His Aim and Work.* Syracuse: C. W. Bardeen, 1889.

Graubard, A. *Free the Children: Radical Reform and the Free School Movement.* New York: Pantheon, 1972.

Ozman, Howard A., and Craver, Samuel M. *Philosophical Foundations of Education.* Columbus, Ohio: Charles E. Merrill, 1981.

Ravitch, D. *The Troubled Crusade: American Education 1945-1980.* New York: Basic Books, 1983.

Rousseau, J. J. *Emile.* New York: Everyman's Library, 1955.

Silberman, Charles. *Crisis in the Classroom.* New York: Random House, 1970.

Tager, Florence. "Politics and Culture in Anarchist Education: The Modern School of New York and Stelton 1911-1915," *Curriculum Inquiry* 16:4 (1986), pp. 391-416.

Troyat, Henri. *Tolstoy.* New York: Crown Publishers, Harmony Books, 1980.

Von Marenholz-Bulow, Bethe. *Reminiscences of Friedrich Froebel.* Boston: Lee and Shepard, 1895.

Weiner, Leo, translator. *Tolstoy on Education.* Chicago: University of Chicago Press, 1967.

5

Intuitive Connections

At the beginning of the book I offered the following definition of holistic education:

> The focus of holistic education is on relationships — the relationship between linear thinking and intuition, the relationship between mind and body, the relationships between various domains of knowledge, the relationship between the individual and community, and the relationship between self and Self. In the holistic curriculum the student examines these relationships so that he/she gains both an awareness of them and the skills necessary to transform the relationships where it is appropriate.

The second part of this book explores these connections.

Linear Thinking and Intuition

The holistic curriculum attempts to restore a balance between linear thinking and intuition. In this chapter I discuss intuition and how we can attempt to link it with linear cognition. Intuition is a complex phenomenon and I devote considerable space to discussing its nature and how we can use various techniques such as metaphor and visualization to enhance its role in the classroom.

Mind and Body (Chapter 6)

The holistic curriculum explores the relationship between mind and body so the student senses the connection between the two. The relationship can be explored by movement, dance, and yoga.

Knowledge/Subject Relationships (Chapter 7)

There are many different ways we can connect academic disciplines and school subjects. For example, Waldorf education connects subject through the arts. The relationship between self and subject matter is also examined, as well as the connection between subject matter and community. I also discuss holistic approaches to thinking that can link subjects.

Community and self (Chapter 8)

The holistic curriculum sees the student in relation to community. Community refers to the school community, the community of one's town and nation, and the global community. The student develops interpersonal skills, community service skills, and social action skills.

Self and self (Chapter 9)

Ultimately the holistic curriculum allows us to realize our true nature. In this chapter I shall discuss Steiner's concept of development, meditation, and world religions as vehicles for this process.

Logic–Intuition

The holistic curriculum connects linear thought and intuition. Recently, there has been a great deal of focus on right and left brain learning. Although this research is interesting, I do not believe it should be the focus for connecting conceptual thought and intuition. First, the right-brain, left-brain theme has been overworked, and the educational connections to the brain research are often not well grounded. Second, there is the danger of getting caught in physiological reductionism, by attempting to link all knowing to the brain. From a holistic perspective it is possible to see the whole human body, including the smallest cell, as learning, growing, and developing.

What Is Intuition?

Intuition is a direct knowing. In contrast, linear cognition involves a sequential, observable process. Noddings and Shore (1984) characterize intuition as "seeing without glasses, hearing without filters, touching with ungloved hand. The immediate character of intuition does not imply accuracy, rightness, or moral goodness. It does imply commitment and clarity" (p. 57). In the intuitive mode there is no mediator. Noddings and Shore derive their view of intuition from Kant and Schopenhauer. From Kant comes the view of intuition as direct knowing and from Schopenhauer the idea that intuition is linked to the will. For Noddings and Shore, the will is the "dynamic centre of self — the heart of being" (p. 59); in other words, it is similar to what I have referred to as the Self or Centre. The will directs intuition and "subordinates analytic and algorithmic activity to its needs, quieting the continual humming of the internal logic machine" (p. 59).

Levels of Intuition

Frances Vaughn (1979) has described four levels of intuition — the physical, emotional, intellectual, and spiritual. The *physical* level of intuition is characterized by a strong bodily response; for example, the awareness that people in the jungle can have when they sense physical danger. Physical intuition, however, differs from instinct in that the person is fully conscious while instinct is more unconscious. Intuitions at this level are also related to the body–mind connection. For example, the body will give the first clues that a person is experiencing stress. Muscle tension or muscle spasms can indicate that the person needs to examine the sources of stress in his or her life.

Vaughn argues that we should learn to trust the responses of our body. A study by Charles Tart (1973) supports this conclusion. In this experiment a subject in a soundproof chamber was asked to tap a telegraph key when he felt he had gotten a "subliminal stimulus." This subject was not given a direct stimulus, but in another soundproof room a person was receiving a low-level electric shock. This second person tried to send a telepathic message to the first person each time he received a shock so that he or she would strike the telegraph key. Interestingly, the key taps were unrelated to the mental messages but bodily responses were related to the mental messages. Brain-wave and heart-rate measurements indicated that the first person was responding to the messages, although he was not conscious of it.

At the *emotional* level the person experiences intuition through feelings. For example, we can pick up "vibrations" from people we meet. Sometimes these feelings can be quite intense, other times they can be more subtle. Vaughn claims that what we refer to as woman's intuition is the emotional level, although this is largely a culturally imposed view of intuition. An example of emotional intuition is given by Vaughn (1979):

> When I was in graduate school a friend of mine had told me how much he wanted to get to know one of our professors whom he greatly admired. One night he dreamed that he was talking to him, but the professor did not say much, and refused to take off his overcoat. As my friend reflected on what the dream was telling him, he realized that he had felt intuitively that this man had wanted to keep his distance ever since they met. Repeated attempts to get better acquainted were of no avail. He later regretted the time and effort expended, for he had "known" all along that it would be fruitless. (p. 71)

Sometimes emotional intuition can be the source of artistic expression, even though it is difficult to describe the connection between the original intuition and its final expression. Elizabeth Herron (1976), a contemporary poet, describes the difficulties of expressing her intuitive insights:

> I was depressed. The world had gone flat and colorless. I had withdrawn. I was a tiny kernel inside my body, adrift amid necessities and obligations, oppressed by my separatedness, cut off from the wellsprings of my soul. I walked up to the pond, took off my clothes and plunged into the water — a sudden shock, cold against my skin. Floating to the surface, I heard a bird call across the meadow. Suddenly, I was at the stillpoint. The bird's call was my voice. We were separate and yet one. I was out there and in here. . . . All things converged in me and radiated from me. "The Center of the circle is everywhere, the circumference nowhere." I recognized this, knowing it had always been so, though I had been cut off from my experience of it. My head filled with poetic images. The dimension of the infinite was everywhere.

> This was a repetition of similar experiences. It is a paradoxical awareness. In these moments I know. But my knowing is not enough. I must struggle to comprehend what I know. My intuitive knowledge must be expressed in order to be communicated. I cannot share my experience merely by telling you about it. As a poet, I seek words for my experience, but words alone are not enough. There are realities — nuances of feeling and meaning, for which words are inadequate."

At the *mental* level intuition is often expressed through images. Here we may have flashes of insight that can lead to scientific inquiry. David Bohm describes a high level of mental intuition as insight. For Bohm (1981) insight is "an act of perception permeated with intense energy and passion, that brings about great clarity . . . This perception includes new forms of imagination and new orders of reason" (p. 15). Bohm states that "Those who knew Einstein will agree that his work was permeated with great passion" (p. 54). Einstein's passionate insight led him to move beyond the existing Newtonian paradigm to develop the theory of relativity.

One of the vehicles for intuitive insight is the mental image. Einstein (1945) said: "The words or the language, as they are written or spoken, do not seem to play any role in my mechanism of thought. The physical entities which seem to serve as elements in thought are certain signs and more or less clear images which can be 'voluntarily' reproduced and combined" (p. 142). Einstein believed that objective reality can only be truly grasped by intuition not by empiricism or logic. Muller-Markus (1976) says: "An idea like Planck's quantam of action was not logically entailed by experiment, nor could it be derived from previous theories. Planck conceived it out of his own self" (p. 154).

Vaughn claims that the "aha" experience of insight is another example of mental intuition. Sometimes the "aha" experience can involve an insight into one's own behavior, or alternatively it can involve a creative solution to a problem. Melvin Calvin (1976), a Nobel Laureate in Chemistry, gives the following example of mental intuition:

> One day I was waiting in my car while my wife was on an errand. I had had for some months some basic information from the laboratory which was incompatible with everything which, up until then, I knew about the photosynthetic process. I was waiting, sitting at the wheel, most likely parked in the red zone, when the recognition of the missing compound occurred. It occurred just like that — quite suddenly — and suddenly, also, in a matter of seconds, the cyclic character of the path of carbon became apparent to me, not in the detail which ultimately was elucidated, but the original recognition of phosphoglyceric acid, and how it got there, and how the acceptor might be regenerated, all occurred in a matter of 30 seconds. (p. 2)

The highest level of intuition is the *spiritual*. Here intuition is independent from feelings, thoughts, and sensations. Vaughn (1979) comments: "Paradoxically, the cues on which intuition depends on the other levels are regarded as interference at this level" (p. 77). James Bugental (1976) has said that "Man knows God in his deepest intuitions about his own nature" (p. 296). At the spiritual level intuition moves beyond dualism to experience unity directly. The following statement by Teilhard de Chardin (1965) is an example of spiritual intuition.

> . . . The farther and more deeply we penetrate into matter, by means of increasingly powerful methods, the more we are confounded by the interdependence of its parts. Each element of the cosmos is positively woven from all the others. . . . It is impossible to cut into this network, to isolate a portion without it becoming frayed and unravelled at all its edges. All around us, as far as the eye can see, the universe holds together, and only one way of considering it is really possible, that is, to take it as a whole, in one piece. (pp. 43-44)

Meditation is a technique designed to quiet the mind so that spiritual intuition can arise. Meditative techniques will be discussed in chapter 9.

Intuition and Education

Why should we focus on intuition in education and seek to balance analytic thought with intuitive insight? First, there is some evidence that intuition is integral to creativity. Wallas (1926) describes four basic elements in the creative process. The first step is *preparation*, where the individual gathers information relevant to the problem or project. At the second stage, *incubation*, the individual relaxes and does not make an effort to work consciously on the problem. Instead, it is suggested that the images realign themselves in the individual as he or she consciously attends to something else. In the *illumination* state the solution will occur often spontaneously and unexpectedly, as in case of the chemist Melvin Calvin. The second and third stages, then, are the intuitive, while the third and fourth stages are more analytical. The fourth stage is *verification,* or *revision*, where the individual puts the idea into use and consciously works with the idea in a more detailed manner.

The Wallas model and other models of creative thinking are useful to the educator in balancing analysis and insight in classroom pedagogy. Visualization, meditation, and various aesthetic experiences can be used to enhance incubation and illumination, while logical problem-solving models (Ross and Maynes, 1982) can be used to facilitate preparation and verification. Effective thinking, then, involves both intuition and analysis. Einstein and Mozart are examples of individuals who were able to relate both analysis and insight effectively at the highest level. If our thinking is dominated by one mode, it is much less effective. If the emphasis is on linear, analytic thinking, we can become plodding in our approach and lose spontaneity in dealing with problems. If we stress the intuitive, then we can lose our ground. Our ideas can become irrelevant if we make no attempt to verify them. Generally, schools have not emphasized the teaching of thinking skills (Ross and Maynes, 1982, p. 2), and when they have, it has usually been linear problem-solving rather than a more holistic approach.

Another reason for an intuitive pedagogy is the research by Jerome Singer (1976), which suggests that the risks of an undeveloped imagination include "delinquency, violence, overeating and the use of dangerous drugs" (p. 32). According to Singer's research, this tendency appears early in children who are impulsive, who are excessively dependent, and who lack a developed inner life. Children who can use their imagination tend to be more relaxed and independent in their behavior. This trend continues into adolescence. Another study revealed that in a child guidance clinic, imaginative children were less likely to be violent. Like the other children in the clinic, they were emotionally troubled, but they exhibited their difficulties in less aggressive ways than their unimaginative peers. These studies indicate that those individuals with an underdeveloped inner life seem to be more vulnerable to external stimuli. Thus, a developed inner life connected to intuition and imagination can be a source of autonomy.

Andrew Weil (1972) has also done research which supports Singer, and he comes up with an even more radical hypothesis when he argues that intuitive consciousness, or what he calls non-linear consciousness, is "an innate, normal drive, analagous to hunger or the sexual drive" (p. 19). According to Weil, if there is not a chance to express our non-linear consciousness we can resort to drug and alcohol abuse. He suggests that the need to explore non-linear consciousness begins early in life, young children often like to "whirl themselves into vertiginous stupors." Children also hyperventilate and have other children squeeze them around until they almost faint. They may even choke each other to lose consciousness. As they get older, children become interested in dreams and the space between waking and sleeping. They can also begin to explore non-rational stages of consciousness through chemical means. This can involve sniffing glue and cleaning fluids. An operation, with its introduction to anesthesia, can also trigger interest in non-linear consciousness, becoming one of the most vivid memories of early childhood. As children sense that the culture does not accept their interest in non-linear consciousness, they may take the interest underground. Exploring the inner life becomes a private experience which is shared only with their most intimate friends.

Weil (1972) observed this developmental trend in working with individuals who had drug problems that were treated at Harvard University. He summarizes this trend by referring to his own life:

> I feel confident about this developmental scheme for two reasons. First, I have seen it clearly in the histories of many hundreds of drug users I have interviewed and known. Second, I have experienced it myself, I was an avid whirler and could spend hours collapsed on the ground with the world spinning around — this despite the obvious unpleasant side effects of nausea, dizziness, and sheer exhaustion (the only aspects of the experience visible to grownups). From my point of view these effects were incidental to a state of consciousness that was extraordinarily fascinating — more interesting than any other state except the one I entered at the verge of sleep. I soon found out that my spinning made grownups upset; I learned to do it with other neighborhood children in out-of-the-way locations, and I kept it up until I was nine or ten. At about the age of four, like most members of my generation, I had my tonsils out, and the experience of ether anesthesia (administered by the old-fashioned open-drop method) remains one of my strongest memories of early life. It was frightening, intensely interesting, and intimately bound up with my thought about death. Some years later I discovered that a particular brand of cleaning fluid in the basement of my house gave me a similar experience, and I sniffed it many times, often in the company of others my age. I could not have explained what I was doing to anyone; the experience was interesting rather than pleasant, and I knew it was important to me to explore its territory. (pp. 24-25)

Intuition in the Classroom

There are several ways in which we can build intuition into our pedagogy and in the rest of this chapter I discuss two methods — visualization and metaphor.

Visualization

Visualization can be seen as a particular type of meditation where the person uses a set of images in either a directed or undirected way. In directed visualization, sometimes referred to as guided fantasy, the person, in the mind's eye, follows a particular set of images. For example, the individual can imagine himself or herself climbing a mountain. The mountain climb is often symbolic of psychological and spiritual growth. In the undirected visualization the person may start with a few general guidelines and then wait for images to appear. Undirected visualization can be used in problem-solving.

Research indicates the positive effects of visualization. The Simontons (1978) have done research which indicates that visualization has helped cancer patients. Their studies show that visualization increases the quality of life, lengthens life expectancy, and in a small percentage of cases may have contributed to remission of the disease. Other studies (Samuels and Samuels, 1975) indicate that visualization is helpful in overcoming the effects of stress. Systematic desensitization is a technique that employs visualization to help people overcome phobias. The person will imagine themselves in the stressful situation (for example, the dentist's office), but dealing with the stress in a more relaxed manner.

Visualization has been used a great deal in sports. Studies have indicated that it is helpful in improving performance. Richardson (1969) has done a study which shows the effects of visualization on the free throws of basketball players. There were three groups in the study and none of the individuals had practised visualization before. One group practised free throws everyday for twenty days. A second group made free throws only on the first and twentieth days with no practice in between. The third group made free throws on the first and twentieth days but spent twenty minutes each day visualizing sinking baskets. The results are interesting. The first group, the one that actually practised, improved 24 percent between the first and last days. The second group, the one that did not practice, did not improve at all. However, the third group, the one that did the visual practice, improved 23 percent between the first and last days. Richardson found that it was important for the visualizer to control the image. For example, one study group which had trouble visualizing bouncing the ball did not improve as much as the others did.

As noted earlier, undirected imagery can be helpful in the creative process. In Wallas's model the illumination phase often occurs through imagery. Ainsworth-Land (1982) has described the relationship between imagery and creativity in a developmental manner. Ainsworth-Land describes first order imaging as sense-related and arising from physical need. The creative product at this level is usually realistic and concrete. Second order imaging is more predictable and often involves improvement of an existing idea or artistic product. Analysis and evaluation are often second order imaging processes. The goal is also clear and may involve curing cancer, stopping smoking, or overcoming the effects of stress. Synthesis is usually found in third order creativity and imagery. Here the product is not just a revision or modification as in second order creativity, but involves something novel. Thus, there is a breakthrough to a new level of thinking. The fourth and final level of creativity and imaging involves the "ultimate form of relatedness" (p. 17). Ainsworth-Land states: "One's whole being comes into play with the conscious and unconscious minds, reason and intuition, inner and outer, subsumed into a kind of meta-consciousness" (p. 17). The poet Blake called this order "four-fold vision" as the persons sometimes feel that they are being guided by a force greater than themselves. The four levels of imagery and creativity are shown in the accompanying table. (p. 12).

Table 1/Developmental Integration of Creativity and Imaging

Imaging		Creativity	
Orders	Self-Involvement	Product	Processes
1st order → spontaneous, sense-based, concrete, direct representation, realistic	non-awareness of "self," creating out of need, survival motivation, "self-creating"	realistic, concrete representation, discovery learning memory building, invention	perceiving, exploring, spontaneous acting
2nd order → comfortable; predictable; awareness of ability to manipulate and control, analogical, comparative	belonging, self-extension; goal directing, ego building and verifying, self-consciousness	improvements and modifications, impressions, strengthening and enhancing, analogical	categorizing, comparing, analyzing, evaluating
3rd order → abstract, symbolic, superimposing, metaphorical, controlled and spontaneous	sharing differences, "selves" realization and re-integration, giving up rigid control, opening to "flow"	innovation, integrated synthesis of old and new abstractions, symbols	abstracting, synthesizing, metaphorical thinking, intuiting
4th order → renunciation of control, chaotic, psychedelic, illuminating receptivity to unconscious material	self as part of larger reality, "meta-consciousness," disintegration of barriers: conscious-unconscious	invention of new order, new paradigm, philosophical shifts, new pattern formation, "inspired" creations	disintegrating, surrendering accepting, opening, building new perceptual order

Visualization and the Classroom

Visualization can be used to facilitate relaxation, to help motivate student interest in subject matter, to facilitate creative writing, and to enhance creativity. I shall give an example in each of these areas in the following sections. (There are others in my book *The Compassionate Teacher*.)

In doing visualization in the classroom, you should let the students know that they are in control of their own images. There is no right "image" for the visualization, since the images will differ for each person. If the student finds it hard to visualize, he or she should just relax and listen to visualization. If an image appears that makes the student frightened or tense, he or she should just open the eyes.

Relaxation

Lie down on the ground and close your eyes. Focus for a few seconds on your breath feeling relaxed with each exhalation. We will now begin to relax each part of the body and we start this process by tensing the muscles in the body and then relaxing them. Begin first with the feet — tense the muscles in the feet, hold the tension for a few seconds and then let go. Now repeat this with the ankles and calf muscles — tighten, hold, and let go. Feel the body becoming relaxed as you do this. Now concentrate on the thigh muscles — tighten, hold, and let go. Move to the buttocks — tighten, hold, and let go. Focus now on the abdomen — tighten, hold, and let go. Now move to the chest muscles — tighten, hold, and let go. Focus on the shoulders — tighten, hold, and let go. Feel the body relax. Tighten the arms now, hold, and let go. Move to the neck — tighten, hold, and let go. Now tighten the facial muscles, hold, and let go. Finally, tighten the whole body, hold, and let go.

Now visualize yourself on an elevator that is descending. As the elevator goes down feel yourself becoming calm and relaxed. I will count down from five to one and as I count down see yourself in the elevator descending and relaxing. Five . . . Four . . . Three . . . Two . . . One. Now you emerge from the elevator and you walk into an open field. It is warm and sunny. You walk for a while and then decide to lie down in the soft, fresh grass.

As you lie there, visualize around your heart a pure white light. This light is full of warmth and energy. Now see the light expand gradually throughout your body and as it expands you feel relaxed and energized . . . Know that anytime you can connect with this light and energy. Open your eyes now, feeling refreshed and energized.

Motivation/Subject Matter

Visualization can be used to motivate student interest in a particular subject or topic. For example, one teacher used visualization to help students understand how a combustion engine works. The following exercise is from Gordon and Poze's (1972) *Teaching Is Listening:*

> You are the piston of an internal combustion engine. You do all the work. You suck in the air and gasoline mixture. You compress it so that it will burn with more power. You're the one that's exploded down when the mixture ignites. You turn the crankshaft and you do the cleaning up. You force out the burnt gases so that everything is ready for the next cycle. Describe what your "piston body" experiences as you go through the four cycles of internal combustion. (pp. 85-86)

Another example is to have students visualize magnetic fields around a transformer. The students can imagine themselves as electrons in the wire of the coil and experience the movement generated by the rapidly changing force field. Then the students can visualize themselves as electrons moving faster and faster as the two fields surrounding the coils are interacting and coming closer.

A third example of a visualization used to enhance interest and motivation in subject matter is to have students imagine themselves as white blood cells moving through the circulatory system in the human body. First, they visualize the arteries throughout the body and travelling to different parts and then being recirculated through the heart. The students can also imagine the white cells and their role in the immune system in fighting disease.

The above examples are from science. It is also possible to have students use imagery in language and the social studies. In social studies the students could imagine themselves as an historical figure facing a particular choice and visualizing the thoughts and emotions that accompanied the decision. The students could also visualize themselves as a loyalist coming to Canada and imagining the thoughts and feelings as the loyalist begins his/her life in a new country.

Creative Writing

One of the best uses of visualization in the classroom is to use it in connection with creative writing as it can be a rich source of ideas. Below is one example from Williams (1983):

> Select a piece of music that evokes strong images for you. Play it for the class (after a relaxation exercise and suitable introduction) and ask them to let the music suggest images, moods, feelings, and sensations to them. Tell them to be receptive to whatever comes to them as the music plays. Afterward, ask them to talk or write about the experience in either prose or poetry. You can start with prose and select the strongest images to form the basis for poetry; or one or two strong images may serve as the basis for a longer prose piece. This fantasy can also be used as a stimulus for an art project. If you use it for both visual and verbal expression, you might devote some class time to discussing how the experiences differed (some students will prefer writing, others painting; it's a matter of personal style). (p. 133)

Imagination improves with practice. Generally, the more students use it the more varied their ideas and the more comfortable they feel with the process. A good source of visualization exercises for elementary school children is *Spinning Inward* by Maureen Murdock (1982). The following one can be used for creative writing:

> Close your eyes and focus your attention on your breath. Gently breathe in . . . and . . . out. As you breathe quietly and calmly, your body becomes more and more relaxed. Now imagine that you are sitting outside in the grass and it's a beautiful warm sunny day. You enjoy looking at all of the new spring flowers. You enjoy their colors and smells. All of a sudden you see a little person in front of you, climbing up the stem of a lovely white daisy. This person is no bigger than your middle finger and turns to you and motions to you to follow. You realize that you, yourself, have become little and you hurry to follow your new friend. You now have three minutes of clocktime equal to all of the time you need to have an adventure with this flower fairy. (after three minutes) Now it is time to say goodbye to your friend and to come back here filled with the memories of your adventure. I will count to 10. Please join me at the count of 6 and open your eyes feeling alert and refreshed at the count of 10. (p. 106)

Metaphor

Another tool for enhancing intuition is metaphor. Metaphorical thinking involves making connections between two words or ideas that are not normally related to one another; however, the two ideas do share some commonality. For example, the human kidney is like a fuel filter in that both screen out certain molecules. Of course, there are significant differences between the fuel filter and the kidney but a discussion of similarities and differences can lead to a more complete understanding of both. Other examples of the metaphor include:

> "a revolution can be compared to a volcano (pressure building toward explosion), narrative writing to a chain with the transitions being the links, theme and variation to the Thanksgiving turkey and the endless ways of preparing its leftovers, and electricity to water running through pipes" (Williams, 1983, p. 56).

Metaphorical teaching asks the students to explore connections and make intuitive leaps in making these connections. W. J. J. Gordon (1966) has described different levels of role-taking in metaphoric thinking. At the first level the person merely describes an object by drawing out the obvious similarities between the two objects or ideas. At the next level the person describes emotions that arise from identifying the similarities. At the third level the student makes an empathetic identification with a living thing. Gordon (1966) gives the example of a student imagining himself or herself as a crab:

> O.K. I'm a fiddler crab. I've got armor all around me — my tough shell. You'd think I could take it easy, but I can't. And that big claw of mine! Big deal! It looks like a great weapon, but it's a nuisance. I wave it around to scare everyone, but I can hardly carry it. Why can't I be big and fast and normal like other crabs? No kidding! That claw doesn't even scare anyone! (p. 24)

The fourth level involves empathetic identification with a non-living object.

Traditional Approach

Eggs   Seeds

Metaphorical Approach

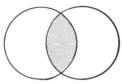

Eggs   Seeds

Figure 2/In the traditional approach, knowledge is separated into categories and each subject presents itself as something entirely new to be learned. Metaphorical teaching emphasizes connections — how the subject is like something already understood. The area where the circles overlap represents how seeds and eggs are alike, e.g., they have many of the same needs, similar parts, similar patterns of development. In these areas, students' understanding of eggs can be applied to the new material they must learn.

(Williams, 1983, p. 59)

There are several advantages to using metaphor. The most obvious from a holistic perspective is that it encourages the student to draw connections between ideas and subject matter. Williams's graph of metaphor is congruent with the diagram of holistic education given in the Introduction. Here she contrasts the traditional approach, which can be compared to the transmission position, with the metaphorical approach, which is similar to the transformation or holistic position. In the traditional approach seeds and eggs are seen as unrelated while in the holistic approach the intersecting circles represent the points where we can make connections.

Metaphor not only encourages the student to make connections but to see patterns. In comparing revolutions to volcanos the student must examine the patterns and principles common to both and then make the connection between the two. The most powerful connections between the components of a metaphor are not similar details but similar principles, as in the example of the kidney and the fuel filter. The student must understand the underlying function of each object to see the connection.

Another advantage of the metaphor is that it is open-ended and provokes inquiry. Metaphors by their very nature encourage questions since there are rarely ready-made answers to metaphoric inquiry. For example, in comparing X and Y we first have to inquire into the nature of each and then draw comparisons.

How can one use metaphor in the classroom? Williams (1983) has suggested the following set of procedures:

1. Decide exactly what you want to teach and what general principle is involved (questions 1 to 4).
2. Generate metaphors, select the one which best communicates the concept you've chosen to teach, and clarify the discrepancies, that is, the ways in which the metaphor does not fit the subject (questions 5 to 9).
3. Make a lesson plan which includes how you'll elicit metaphors from students (question 10-, especially part 3). (p. 63)

Below is an example of the procedures put into practice.

1. What do I want students to know about the kidney?
    How they function and their importance to the body.
2. How do they function?
    They filter wastes.
3. How do they filter wastes?
    They sort molecules: Some pass through, some are retained. (In an advanced class you might want to be even more specific about this point.)
4. What's their importance to the body?
    They remove wastes so the blood can carry more nutrients and pick up more wastes.
5. What can I think of that filters wastes by sorting out something (in other words, that functions like a kidney)?
    (At this point just sit and let ideas come to you. Don't force them; be receptive to images or vaguely formed ideas.)
    A fuel filter, or a coffee filter for that matter.
    Different kinds of sorters — a gravel screen, an egg sorter, an IBM card sorter that selects any card that has a certain pattern of holes punched on it.

A parking lot where cars with certain stickers are admitted.

School games where you need a student body card to get in.

6. All my metaphors are sorters. Do any of them purify a circulating system?

    The fuel filter does.

7. Is everyone in the class familiar enough with a fuel filter to understand the metaphor?

    No.

8. Okay, we can still use it to clarify things later, but let's find a clear metaphor to introduce the idea.

    How about a gravel sorter? I can demonstrate that so that they can see how the sorting works. If I can't get that, I can use a coffee filter, though I'll have to make it clear that the kidneys don't sort on the basis of solids versus liquids.

9. How is the gravel sorter different from the kidneys?

    It's not part of a circulating system.

    Its sorting is much simpler than the kidneys; the gravel sorter uses the sole criterion of size, while the kidney uses much more complex criteria.

10. How do I put this all together?

    First, I'll use the gravel sorter or coffee filter to introduce the concept of sorting and separating and will explore how the metaphor fits and how it doesn't (degree of complexity in criteria for sorting, not part of circulating system).

    I'll talk about other sorters and ask students for examples. We'll compare their sorters to kidneys. I'll ask for examples of sorters that purify a circulating system. If they have trouble, I can ask for examples of circulating systems and then ask them to find the thing in the system that filters wastes. If necessary, I can suggest the fuel filter or the swimming pool filter. (pp. 62-63)

Metaphors can sometimes be used at the beginning of a lesson to stimulate interest in the material. One teacher (Williams, 1983, p. 69) began his class on the French Revolution by examining the power structure of the school. Once the students saw how power functioned in their own institution, they became more interested in the power struggles in eighteenth-century France. Williams notes: "Instead of memorizing the Three Estates and the roles each played, students looked for analogues in the school, explored the power relations between groups, and related them to the situation in France" (p. 69).

Metaphors can also be used in testing. Again the answer to a metaphoric question on a test will not be scorable with a simple checklist, but instead will ask the teacher to assess the student's reasoning and the connections that he or she draws. Below is an example:

1. List the major events leading up to the French Revolution and explain their importance.
2. How was the period leading up to the French Revolution like the building up of a thunderstorm? Be sure to include in your analogy the major events leading up to the Revolution. (p. 71)

Metaphor can also be used to stimulate creative writing. The following questions are from Gordon's (1968) Synectics approach:

1. What *MACHINE* acts like *a SPLINTER GOING INTO YOUR FINGER?* (p. 8)
2. How is a *BEAVER CHEWING ON A LOG* like a *TYPEWRITER?* (p. 8)
3. What *ANIMAL* is like a *PARACHUTE?* (p. 9)
4. What *THING IN THE KITCHEN* is like a *BEAVER?* (p. 9)

Metaphor can also be combined with imagery to encourage creative thinking. For example, Williams suggests the following activity where the teacher begins by taking the students on a guided fantasy where they are in a garden of roses. The students visualize seeing, touching, and smelling the red rose. While their eyes are still closed the teacher then reads Burns's *My Love Is Like a Red, Red Rose.* After the reading the students discuss the experience and how it might differ with a different flower or even with a different colored rose.

Summary

Intuition involves direct knowing and occurs at different levels — physical, emotional, intellectual, spiritual. Intuition needs to be integrated into the classroom because it can enhance the student's thinking, particularly creative problem-solving. Two different strategies for enhancing intuition were discussed in this chapter — visualization and metaphor.

References

Ainsworth-Land, Vaune. "Imagining and Creativity: An Integrating Perspective." *The Journal of Creative Behavior,* 16 (1982), 5-28.

Bohm, David. "Insight, Knowledge, Science and Human Values." In *Toward the Recovery of Wholeness,* edited by Douglas Sloan. New York: Teachers College Press, 1981, 1984.

Bugental, James. *The Search for Existential Identity.* San Francisco: Josey Bass, 1976.

Calvin, Melvin. "Dialogue: Your Most Exciting Moment in Research?" *LBL Magazine.* Fall, 1976.

de Chardin, Teilhard. *The Phenomenon of Man,* pp. 43-44. New York: Harper Torch Books, 1965.

de Mello, Anthony. *Sadhana: A Way to God.* New York: Image Books, 1978.

Gordon, W. J. J. *The Metaphorical Way of Knowing.* Cambridge, Mass.: Porpoise Books, 1966.

Gordon, W. J. J. *Making It Strange.* New York: Harper and Row, 1968.

Herron, Elizabeth. Unpublished paper, 1976.

Miller, John. *The Compassionate Teacher.* Englewood Cliffs, N.J.: Prentice-Hall, 1981.

Muller-Markus, Siegfried. "The Structure of Creativity in Physics. In *Vistas in Physical Reality,* edited by E. Laszlo and E. Sellon. New York: Seldon Press, 1976.

Murdock, Maureen. *Spinning Inward: Using Guided Imagery with Children.* Culver City, Ca.: Peace Press, 1982.

Noddings, Nel, and Shore, Paul, J. *Awakening the Inner Eye: Intuition in Education.* New York: Teachers College Press, 1984.

Richardson, A. *Mental Imagery.* New York: Springer Publishing Co., 1969.

Ross, John, and Maynes, Florence. *Teaching Problem Solving.* Toronto: OISE Press, 1982.

Samuels, Mike, and Samuels, Nancy. *Seeing with the Mind's Eye: The History, Techniques and Uses of Visualization.* New York: Random House, 1975.

Simonton, Carl, and Matthews-Simonton, Stephanie. *Getting Well Again: A Step-by-Step, Self-Help Guide to Overcoming Cancer of Patients and Their Families.* Los Angeles, Ca.: Tarcher, 1978.

Singer, Jerome. "Fantasy, the Foundation of Serenity." *Psychology Today,* July 1976.

Tart, Charles. "The Physical Universe, the Spiritual Universe and the Paranormal." In *Transpersonal Psychologies,* edited by Charles Tart. New York: Harper and Row, 1975.

Vaughn, Frances. *Awakening Intuition.* Garden City, N.J.: Anchor Books, 1979.

Wallas, G. *The Art of Thought.* London: Watts, 1926.

Weil, Andrew. *The Natural Mind.* Boston: Houghton Mifflin, 1972.

Williams, Linda Verlee. *Teaching for the Two-Sided Mind.* Englewood Cliffs, N.J.: Prentice-Hall, 1983.

6

Body-Mind Connection

Wilder Penfield, the Canadian Neurosurgeon and brain researcher, found that our awareness (the mind) is not located in any particular part of the brain but, in fact, directs the brain. According to Penfield (1975), our mind ''seems to focus attention. The mind is aware of what is going on. The mind reasons and makes new decisions. It understands, it acts as though endowed with an energy of its own, it can make decisions and put them into effect by calling upon various brain mechanisms'' (pp. 75-76, 80). However, it is also possible for the brain to run on ''automatic pilot'' without the conscious awareness of the mind. When this happens, the body–mind connection can be broken.

James Lynch (1985) has been studying the relation between mind and body and has found that many people suffering from hypertension are not aware of their body messages. For example, when their heart is beating at a high rate, they are not conscious of their heart pounding. Lynch also found that people who suffer from migraines often experience a drop in blood pressure and have cold hands before the onset of a migraine; however, the patient will be unaware of such bodily changes.

According to Lynch, hypertension is the major health problem in the United States. It is estimated that between forty to sixty million Americans suffer from its effects. Lynch in his studies has found that one of the main reasons for the disease is that the hypertensive person has lost touch with his or her body. The hypertensive's mind does not hear the messages (for example, muscle tension, pounding heart) the body is sending. Lynch conducted his studies of hypertensives while they were talking and he found that their blood pressure tends to rise markedly at this point. Hypertensives also have a hard time listening, as they are preoccupied with what they will be saying next. Consequently their blood pressure does not go down as much as when a normal person is listening. Lynch found that human dialogue is characterized by a rhythm of increased heart beat and blood pressure while talking and lower heart beat and blood pressure while listening. This coincides with the model of the active ego-based mind and the listening Self-based mind presented in the last chapter. Often in talking we are trying to persuade, to manipulate, and to bring the other person in line with the ego's view. While listening, we are less likely to be planning and manipulating; but instead simply relating to the world as it is.

Other researchers have made the same conclusion as Lynch that the psychosomatic patient is not in touch with his/her body and feelings. For example, Friedman and

Sweet (1954) used the term "emotional illiterates" to describe psychosomatic patients who have a difficult time describing their feelings. These patients became bewildered when it was suggested that emotional problems could be contributing to their difficulties. Friedman and Sweet conclude that psychosomatics bury their emotional problems in their body so deeply that they lose their capacity for insight. In other words, they are running on automatic pilot and their conscious awareness is no longer in touch with their bodies and feelings.

Two French psychiatrists, Marty and de M'Uzan (1963), published a paper which indicated that psychosomatic patients showed a paucity of feeling in terms of describing their difficulties as well as a lack of fantasy. Marty and de M'Uzan referred to psychosomatics' responses to questions about their feelings as "operational thinking." They also noted that these patients did not relate their feelings to changes in their bodies but tended to focus on small, trivial details of external events. For example, the normal patient when asked "How do you know you were angry?" will describe their stomach churning or their muscles becoming tense, while the psychosomatic refers to external events.

Building on the work of these investigators, Dr Peter Sifneos (1975) coined the term *alexithymia* to describe the fact that psychosomatic patients are not able to describe their feelings. In another study on alexithymia, Krystal (1979) found that these patients showed a marked impairment in their capacity for creativity and their ability to fantasize. The Krystal research seems to support Singer's research described in the last chapter which indicates that imagination and fantasy are important to the development of wholeness.

In summarizing this research, Lynch concludes that the psychosomatic patient seals himself or herself from others, or what Lynch calls the social membrane. For Lynch real speech involves an invitation of the speaker to enter into his or her consciousness, "that is, into his or her body and ultimately into his or her mind's heart" (p. 243). For the psychosomatic this invitation becomes a threat as "their speech becomes an act of battering or hiding, rather than an invitation" (p. 243).

Lynch argues that there are two primary reasons for the modern problem of hypertension, and particularly the large number of psychosomatics who are cut off from their feelings and their bodies. One is the seventeenth-century movement led by Descartes that tended to see the person as a soul trapped in a machine. According to Lynch (1985), "Descartes removed the Greek idea of logos from living bodies and limited it to a soul that was restricted to the human mind. By separating soul from body, Descartes, in essence, created two realities for humans; one, a machine body; and the other, a mind or soul which interacts both with the machine body as well as with other human beings. Thus, human beings relate to each other in dialogue only through their minds" (pp. 289-90). Lynch notes that it was significant that Descartes' fundamental statement was "I think therefore I am" rather than "I feel therefore I am." If we relate to each other only through our minds, then, human dialogue becomes strictly rational dialogue. According to Lynch, "In this new view, the feeling of love is merely an imprecise thought; loneliness has nothing to do with physical health. . . Descartes made the human body utterly irrelevant to human dialogue" (p. 291).

The second reason for body–mind divisions is our educational system. Lynch argues that school systems emphasize calculus and physics, which require a great deal of training, while feelings are taken for granted. There is "no training, no exercising, no sensitizing — except, that is, for a rational discussion of these human feelings'' (p. 271). He concludes:

> For many students, school systems can become a training ground where they are taught not to understand but rather to control their feelings. For those individuals who are already predisposed to be particularly insensitive to their feelings, and who will subject themselves later in life to serious psychosomatic disorders, the entire experience in schools serves to reinforce their problems. Feelings are seen as an irrational force, a dark side of human nature that must be controlled. The academic lesson is that if you cannot control your feelings, then at least you ought to hide them. Since those attitudes and beliefs coincide with and amplify similar parental dispositions, psychosomatically prone individuals often do well in school. Not sensing feelings and compulsively following structure and rules is precisely the type of behavior that prepares one to do well on objective tests. It allows one to spend endless hours learning minute details from texts while simultaneously denying one's anxiety and anger at having to spend so much time competing with fellow students. (p. 271)

Masters and Houston (1979) come to a similar conclusion when they claim that school leads to inadequate development of the body. They cite the research of Wilfred Barlow (1975), which indicates that most children have a number of physical defects that increase as they grow older. Barlow conducted his research in secondary schools and colleges in England and reached the following conclusions:

> Seventy percent of all boys and girls show quite marked muscular and postural deficiencies. Mostly these defects appear as passing inefficiencies and difficulties in learning; they become accentuated in emotional situations, and they presage an uneasy adolescence in which childhood faults become blown up into full-fledged defects. By the age of eighteen, only 5 percent of the population are free from defects, 15 percent have slight defects, 65 percent have quite severe defects, and 15 percent have very severe defects. These figures are based on my published surveys of boys and girls from secondary schools, and students from physical training, music and drama colleges, some of whom might reasonably be expected to have a higher physical standard than the rest of the population. (p. 15)

We have no reason to believe these figures would be any different in North America. Even physical education programs which are aimed at developing the body can contribute to a lack of integration. Masters and Houston believed that physical exercises should concentrate on developing a person's body image or the ability to connect the body to our consciousness. Unfortunately, many physical education programs focus only on building up either the muscles or the cardiovascular system or both. Masters and Houston conclude that exercises such as ''running and jogging, weight-lifting, rope-skipping, swimming, isometrics, isotonics, and sports in general'' (p. 36) can, in fact, be detrimental. Shelton (1971) agrees:

> There is hardly any form of athletics in which all of the muscles are not brought into play, but when we study their activities we see that some parts of the body are taxed sufficiently to produce considerable development while others are only slightly used. Marvelous control is required in some parts to execute the movements, while others require little or no control. Every game or sport exer-

cises and develops some groups of muscles or some region of the body more than other groups or regions and in time produces more or less deformity if not counter-balanced by other features of the exercise program. The unevenness in the distribution of effort results in uneven development and control. The result is that our athletes are miserable specimens. (p. 37)

The competitive aspect of sports often contributes to athletes overtraining or developing certain parts of their bodies at the expense of the whole body. As I write this, there has been a rash of muscle rib cage injuries in baseball, and these injuries have been attributed to baseball players lifting weights so they can hit more home runs. However, the weightlifting has led to muscle tightness and more injuries.

Two sports often thought to be beneficial are swimming and cycling. However, Bertherat and Bernstein (1977) note that swimming can lead to overdeveloped back muscles while the front of the body can remain underdeveloped. They also conclude that a common effect of cycling is a "tightening of the muscles in the back of the neck and lower back; on the other hand, a loss of tonicity in the abdominal muscles and a compression of the stomach . . . can lead to digestive problems (very common in professional cyclists)" (pp. 58-59)

Psychophysical Re-education

In contrast, Masters and Houston offer a program in psychophysical awareness. This is a program based in part on the work of Alexander (1969) and Feldenkrais (1972) and attempts to connect "words and images to the appropriate movements and sensations" (p. 61). The exercises focus on different parts of the body but most of the exercises include an imagery component to help connect mind and body. The Alexander Technique and the Feldenkrais system of Functional Integration is based on the premise that the body and the nervous system are closely connected. Problems can arise because the body can get the wrong messages from the nervous system. Feldenkrais (1970), however, argues that the body can be re-educated:

> Many of our failings, physical and mental, need not therefore be considered as diseases to be cured, nor an unfortunate trait of character, for they are neither. They are an acquired result of a learned faulty mode of doing. The body only executes what the nervous system makes it do. It moulds itself during growth for a longer period, and to a greater extent, than in any other animal. Actions repeated innumerable times for years on end, such as all our habitual actions, mould even the bones, let alone the muscular envelope. The physical faults that appear in our body long after we were born are mainly the result of activity we have imposed on it. Faulty modes of standing and walking produce flat feet, and it is the mode of standing and walking that must be corrected, and not the feet. The extent to which our frame is able to adjust itself to the use and requirements we make of it seems to be limitless; by learning a better use of control, the feet, the eyes, or whatever organ it may be, will again adjust themselves and change their shape and function accordingly. The transformations that can be produced, and their rapidity, sometimes border on the incredible. (p. 152)

Because the body and mind are so connected it is possible to re-educate the body. According to Masters and Houston, the re-education must start in the motor cortex of the brain. They suggest that when a person's wrist is broken there may occur an inhibition in the motor cortex. This inhibition occurs as a result of the inactivity since the wrist is in a cast or splints. When the cast is removed it may be difficult to move the wrist because of the inhibition in the motor cortex. Masters and Houston suggest that mental exercises could help re-educate the brain so that the accompanying muscle activities can occur more easily. They claim that psychophysical re-education is "neural reeducation which makes the nervous system demonstrably more responsive and amendable to change. Psychophysical exercises are in part effective communications to the brain, specifying bodily changes which the brain can and will effect in response to the appropriate stimulus" (p. 49). Below is a segment from one of the introductory exercises in the book:

> Put your arms down at your sides with the palms of your hands down. And just imagine turning your head from left to right. Imagine it vividly, what it feels like, how far the head goes to each side, and how quickly you do it. Imagine that you fold your arms over your chest and continue to imagine turning the head. Imagine that at least ten times, taking care that you breathe freely as you do it. When you imagined the movement with the arms folded over the chest, did you imagine that the shoulders and the back left the floor? . . . Now with your eyes open, actually turn your head quickly from side to side. Notice whether your shoulders go up and down as the head turns, and do so spontaneously. Then stop, rest, and close your eyes.
> (pp. 97-98)

Psychophysical re-education, then, combines visualization with movement to enhance physical performance and well-being.

Mindfulness

Another technique for connecting mind and body is awareness of movement. Awareness of movement is also employed in various meditative traditions; for example, in Buddhism there is a walking meditation where individuals focus their attention on lifting the foot, moving it, and placing it down. This awareness of the body is described below in an excerpt from the Buddhist *Satipatthana-sutta:*

> "And how, O priests, does a priest live, as respects the body, observant of the body?
>
> ". . . O priests, a priest in walking thoroughly comprehends his walking, and in standing thoroughly comprehends his standing, and in sitting thoroughly comprehends his sitting, and in lying down thoroughly comprehends his lying down, and in whatever state his body may be thoroughly comprehends that state.
> ". . . But again, O priests, a priest, in advancing and retiring has an accurate comprehension of what he does; in looking and gazing has an accurate comprehension of what he does; in drawing in his arm and in stretching out his arm has an accurate comprehension of what he does; in wearing his cloak, his bowl, and his robes has an accurate comprehension of what he does; in eating, drinking, chewing, and tasting has an accurate comprehension of what he does; in easing his bowels and his bladder has an accurate comprehension of what he does; in

walking, standing, sitting, sleeping, waking, talking, and being silent has an accurate comprehension of what he does.'' (Cited in J. Needleman, 1975, pp. 152-53.)

This awareness is called mindfulness and is a result of training one's attention. By being mindful one develops a connectedness with one's body. After practice, the awareness becomes natural, even effortless. Mindfulness lets one become aware of any tension in the body almost immediately. By focussing attention on the stressful area in the body, the individual can relax the affected area so that tension does not build up in the body. Often tension can build up in such areas as the neck and shoulders without our being aware of the stress, and this can eventually affect how we feel and act. However, mindfulness allows the person to deal with tension almost immediately as it arises in the body. The following is a simple exercise which you could do with students to develop mindfulness.

> Start walking very slowly. As you walk be aware as you lift your foot, move it and place it down. Notice any sensations in your body as you do this. Don't force the walking, just be aware of it. After three or four minutes begin to walk a little faster, but continue to be aware of your movement as you lift and move your feet . . . Now start skipping. Skip slowly at first, being aware of the movement with your feet and legs. Also note any feelings and sensations in the body as you skip. Skip now a little faster, but keeping an awareness of your movement . . . Now begin running. Not too fast at first. As much as possible be aware of your running and of your leg movement. Run faster now, keeping as much awareness as possible as you move . . . Now slow the running keeping the awareness focussed on the body. Slow down to a walk again. Keep your awareness on lifting and moving the leg. Now come to a stop.

After the exercise is over, the students can discuss their experiences and whether they were able to keep an awareness throughout the exercise. As noted in the Buddhist text, mindfulness can be applied to all our movements and other exercises can easily be developed with other activities (for example, eating, swimming, writing). Below are two exercises from Hanh's (1976) *The Miracle of Mindfulness* which show how mindfulness can be applied to daily life.

Mindfulness while making tea

Prepare a pot of tea to serve a guest or to drink by yourself. Do each movement slowly, in mindfulness. Do not let one detail of your movements go by without being mindful of it. Know that your hand lifts the pot by its handle. Know that you are pouring the fragrant warm tea into the cup. Follow each step in mindfulness. Breathe gently and more deeply than usual. Take hold of your breath if your mind strays.

Washing the dishes

Wash the dishes relaxingly, as though each bowl is an object of contemplation. Consider each bowl as sacred. Follow your breath to prevent your mind from straying. Do not try to hurry to get the job over with. Consider washing the dishes the most important thing in life. Washing the dishes is meditation. If you cannot wash the dishes in mindfulness, neither can you meditate while sitting in silence. (p. 85)

Movement/Dance

Another vehicle for connecting mind and body is movement and dance. Movement education became more popular in the late 1960s and 1970s, particularly in primary-level classroom. One of the greatest teachers and performers of movement/dance in this century was Isadora Duncan, and her approach to movement is outlined in a recent biography by Fredericka Blair (1986). Isadora was critical of dance that concentrated on technique unconnected to inner feeling. She wrote in her book *The Art of Dance* of "those systems of dancing that are only arranged gymnastics, only too logically understood (Dalcroze, etc.)" (p. 51). Instead, she taught her pupils: "Remember always start your movements from within. The desire to make a certain gesture must be there first" (cited in I. Duncan, n.d., p. 12). John Martin (1947), dance critic for the *New York Times,* spoke of Isadora's "insistence that the exercises of her young pupils . . . never lapse into . . . mere muscular exertion. . . The dancer's habit of moving must be made such that movement is never an end in itself but always the outward result of an inward awareness. It follows then that no series of set movements, whatever their virtues for muscle development, can be established as a training technique." Isadora focussed on natural movements such as walking, running, and skipping, always attempting to connect the outward movement to the inner feeling. The goal of dance, however, was not an expression of personal feeling as much as the expression of universal feelings, coming from the dancer's deepest emotion. In Isadora's words:

> His body is simply the luminous manifestation of his soul. . . . This is the truly creative dancer, natural but not imitative, speaking in movement out of himself and out of something greater than all selves. (1928, p.52)

Isadora did not deny technique, but stressed that it must be integrated with this universal sense. She realized that the dancer must work so that he or she passes through "stages of psychological and physical self-awareness to reach this final stage of self-forgetfulness, of surrendering to the music and the promptings of one's innermost being" (Blair, 1986, p. 49). The means for accessing one's innermost self was music as she danced to compositions of composers such as Beethoven and Gluck. Tobias (1977) summarizes Duncan's approach:

> Duncan created a dance that was motivated, both physically and emotionally, from the center of the body as opposed to a peripheral merely decorative operation of arms and legs — "tricks" as she scornfully called them, that could be taught to the feet. At first glance, her vocabulary looks fairly narrow and simple — based as it is on walks, skips and runs, the upper body moving in complement — but its plasticity and rhythms are remarkably subtle (today's virtuoso professionals are regularly defeated by it), and with it, Duncan was able to create a world of emotion. The repertory she left ranges from the sensual lyricism of the Brahms Waltzes, to a stark monument to grief, Mother, to the brilliant violence of the so-called Revolutionary Etude, in which the body seems alternately to give in to the gravity and lassitude that suggest oppression and defiantly rip itself from its fetters; it poses the gently purity of the Dance of the Blessed Spirits (to Gluck) against the overripe wine-madness of the Bacchanale. . . . Her work is enjoying a surge of interest in the present period when modern dance is looking back over

its history and consolidating its achievements. Duncan's clear, simple, lucidly constructed dances go back to fundamentals of shape, weight and dynamics that contemporary dance has lost touch with in its pursuit of virtuosity.

The *New York Times,* 22 May 1977

In sum, Isadora offers a holistic approach to dance that educators developing movement programs should consider.

Dimonstein (1971) has developed a holistic approach to dance for the elementary schools classroom. The focus of her approach is on developing kinesthetic awareness. Kinesthetic awareness refers to the children's ability to control their movements and to feel the movements at the same time. With gestures they learn to give shape and form to their inner thoughts. Dance, then, is not just acting out, but giving form to, inner feelings through visual images expressed in movement. For example, in exploring the concept of fear, the children find some movement to express their conception of fear. The students can first start with an unstructured visualization where they let images of fear come into their mind. They can then articulate these images or draw them, and finally they can express their image of fear through movement.

Dimonstein describes three stages of movement and dance. At the first stage the student *explores* various movements as they explore physical self with basic movement patterns.

The next level is *improvisation* where students begin to connect inner feelings with movement. At this level they begin to use movement as a form of self-expression, although the students usually have not yet reached the level of dance in which there is definite form to the movements.

At the *dance* level children deepen their perception of inner feelings by giving shape to them through physical activity. In dance there is movement into patterns that express a particular idea or theme. Dance for Dimonstein (1971), however, is not storytelling. Rather it centres on "metaphoric qualities which symbolize forces or objects" (p. 13). The body is the centre in this symbolic processs. Through dance children develop "muscle sense" or kinesthetic perception of bodily movement. In dance they gain a sense of flow and rhythm, as movement is not isolated but is part of a whole. While dancing, the children develop a sense of fluency, as their bodies become more centred. As the children gain this "muscle sense" they learn to express their own feelings and they also learn which movement is appropriate. Dance, then, becomes a vehicle for expressing the inner life of the child.

Waldorf Education/Eurythmy

Rudolf Steiner, the Austrian philosopher, who investigated and developed approaches to so many areas of human endeavor such as farming, architecture, and medicine, is also known for developing Waldorf education. The Waldorf movement, which began in 1919, has become the fastest growing independent school movement in the world. Steiner based his pedagogy on his conception of the human being. This conception led to an emphasis in Waldorf education on his particular form of movement: eurythmy.

Before looking at eurythmy, it is important to examine briefly Steiner's conception of human development. Steiner sees the person as having four "bodies" and believes that each of these bodies should be emphasized at a different time in the child's education.

The first of these bodies is the physical body. It is this body which is dominant during the first seven years of life. The physical environment is very important for the child at this age. It needs to be rich in shape and color and also should offer behaviors which the child can imitate physically. The physical objects should be ones that the child can work with and which stimulate his or her imagination. For example, Steiner recommends that the child make a doll out of a napkin. Singing and movement are also very important at this stage of development. The children will clap out numbers, and dance movements are seen to have strong influence on developing the physical organism.

The second body, the etheric, becomes predominant around the age of seven when children lose their baby teeth. According to Steiner (1975), "the etheric body is a force-form; it consists of active forces, and not of matter" (pp. 13-14). Education during the elementary school years is based on imagination and not the intellect. Steiner (1975) stressed that "it is not abstract ideas that have an influence on the developing etheric body, but living pictures that are seen and comprehended inwardly" (p. 32). Steiner (1975) concludes:

> The etheric body is worked upon through pictures and examples — i.e. by carefully guiding the imagination of the child. As before the age of seven we have to give the child the actual physical pattern for him to copy, so between the time of the change of teeth and puberty, we must bring into his environment things with the right inner meaning and value. For it is from the inner meaning and value of things that the growing child will now take guidance. Whatever is fraught with a deep meaning that works through pictures and allegories, is the right thing for these years. The etheric body will unfold its forces if the well-ordered imagination is allowed to take guidance from the inner meaning it discovers for itself in pictures and allegories — whether seen in real life or communicated to the mind. It is not abstract conceptions that work in the right way on the growing etheric body, but rather what is seen and perceived — not indeed with the outward senses, but with the eye of the mind. This seeing and perceiving is the right means of education for these years. (pp. 29-30)

In the elementary school years Waldorf emphasizes fairy tales, myth, and fable to stimulate the child's imagination. The child should not be rushed into intellectual activity, and mental activity should be complemented with activities such as handwork where the student knits his or her own seat cushion or hat. Writing should be viewed as an imaginative manual activity, and children should have the opportunity to write and tell stories aloud. Children should also have direct experiences with nature and objects instead of becoming too dependent on the written word. Richards (1980) states: "Be careful of mechanizing the processes of reading and writing" (p. 57).

Music is also very important during the elementary years. Music for Steiner (1975) "must bring to the etheric body that rhythm which will then enable it to sense in all things the rhythm otherwise concealed" (p. 42). Other arts such as drawing and drama are important and are often integrated in the main lesson (which will be discussed more fully in the next chapter).

Games and gymnastic exercises are important at this level. Steiner suggested that these exercises must be thought out very carefully so that the etheric body is strengthened within the child. A certain approach to gymnastics called *Bothmer* was developed from Steiner's work by a Count Bothmer. Gymnastics, art, music, storytelling, drama are all designed to nourish the child's soul, which Richards (1980) claims is the central task of Steiner education (p. 59).

The third body of the human being is the "sentient" or "astral" body, which is "the vehicle of pain and pleasure, of impulse, craving, passion, and the like — all of which are absent in a creature consisting only of physical and etheric bodies" (Steiner, 1975, p. 12). The astral body is predominant during adolescence. During this phase Waldorf education hones in on developing the student's critical intelligence. The artistic element is kept but is woven into secondary school subjects with an emphasis on developing intellectual autonomy.

The fourth and final body of the human being is the human ego. Steiner's conception of the ego is really closer to the "Self," as Steiner says the "I" or the "God" begins to speak to the person from within when the fourth body begins to predominate. Steiner (1976) connects the ego to eurythmy in the following passage:

> When I speak a verb my ego joins in with what the physical body of the other person is doing. I unite my ego with the physical body of the other when I speak a verb. Our listening, especially with verbs, is in reality always a participation. What is so far the most spiritual part of man participates, only it suppresses the activity. Only in eurythmy is this activity placed in the external world. In addition to everything else, eurythmy also gives the activity of listening. When one person tells something, the other listens; he performs in his ego what lives physically in the sounds, but he suppresses it. The ego always does eurythmy in participation, and what eurythmy puts before us through the physical body is nothing other than a making visible of listening. So you always do eurythmy when you listen, and when you actually do eurythmy you are just making visible what you leave invisible when you listen. The manifestation of the activity of the listening human being is in fact eurythmy. It is not something arbitrary but rather in reality the revelation of what the listening human being does. (p. 65)

Eurythmy is used at all levels of Waldorf education, although it is probably most important during the elementary years because it is primarily related to activity of the etheric body. Eurythmy is not dance movement or personal expression; instead, it is a physical form of speech. The physical guestures are taken from the movements of the larynx. The arms and hands are very important in eurythmy. Eurythmy can also be performed to music and this is called "tone eurythmy." When I was at the Waldorf school, grade 4 students were doing tone eurythmy by moving to major/minor cords.

In the early grades the children walk and run to form geometrical patterns such as circles, figure eights, squares, triangles, and pentagons. Eurythmy can help the unsocial child learn how to move in time with the other children, and can help the over-intellectual child to step in time to rhythm. Eurythmy can also be combined with storytelling at the primary grades. Harwood (1958) comments:

> If we are going to perform a little story in this sort of eurhythic action, music must also come in. The children begin to feel the qualities of different rhythms
> — perhaps the light anapaest for the prince's horse galloping throught the forest
> — the trochee for the princess lost at night in that same forest and thinking of

the home she will never see again — the spondee for the ogre walking heavily home from his day's marauding. Picture, rhythm and feeling — when these are a unity and realized in movement, education has begun. (p. 151)

Older children can try more complicated movements such as marking the beat with the feet while clapping the rhythm with hands and then reversing the process. Eurythmy can also be practised with rods so that if the movement is not done correctly the student's rod will clash with a neighbor's rod. These exercises, then, develop both control of the body and concentration. As the children in grades 4 and 5 study history, myth, and legends, they can apply their learning to eurythmy. The rhythm of the Norse legends can be compared to Greek mythology. Harwood notes that the "alliterative metre of the North has a deep quality of will in it . . . while the hexameter, on the other hand, is the most harmonious, the most harmonizing of all rhythms" (p. 152). By reading Homer and then doing eurythmy the students gain a much deeper feel for Greek culture than they would through a mere verbal approach.

As the child approaches adolescence, eurythmy can be related to the intellectual development of the student. For example, grammar can be explored through eurythmy as the active and passive tense can be taught through movement. Students at this age can relate more closely to music and eurythmy by having some students play their instruments while the other students do some movements.

Eurythmy is usually taught by a teacher trained in the field, but the classroom teacher is encouraged to take part in the lesson. According to Harwood: "When the eurythmy teacher is as much interested in what the children are learning in their main lessons, as the class teacher in what they are doing in movement, the children thrive in a harmony of mind and will" (p. 154). In secondary school eurythmy can be combined with drama, "perhaps in a play when there are nature spirits, as in Milton's *Comus,* or *A Midsummer Night's Dream*" (p. 155). Harwood concludes by emphasizing the importance of eurythmy in Waldorf:

Of all elements in modern life it is the rhythmical side which is most deficient - a deficiency only too apparent in the arts today. The whole of a Waldorf education is based on rhythm, and may therefore be called curative for an age. But in this rhythmical education there is no doubt where the centre lies. It is in Eurythmy. (p. 155)

Summary

By exploring psychophysical re-education, movement, dance, mindfulness, and eurythmy we can help the student connect mind and body. By connecting mind and body we facilitate human wholeness, a wholeness that is evident in the way James Lynch (1985), unlike the psychosomatic, listens to a fellow human being:

At times I have found myself trembling when meeting the eyes of a patient — looking at me, searching, hoping earnestly to discover for the first time the emotional meaning of his or her elevated blood pressure, rapid heart rate, or freezing hands. At such moments I have felt Schrodinger's reality — deeply felt it — for surely there is far more to their eyes than optical sensors whose only function is to detect light quanta. And I have trembled then precisely because I have caught a glimpse of the infinite universe behind those eyes and the reality of a universal

Logos uniting us in dialogue. And it is at such moments, in the quiet sharing of reason and feelings in dialogue, that I have felt most alive and human. (p. 310)

References

Alexander, F. M. *The Resurrection of the Body.* New York: Delta Books, 1969.

Barlow, W. *The Alexander Principle.* London: Arrow Books, 1975.

Bertherat, T., and Berstein, C. *The Body Has Its Reasons: Anti-Exercises and Self-Awareness.* New York: Pantheon Books, 1977.

Blair, F. *Isadora: Portrait of the Artist as a Woman.* New York: William Morrow, 1986.

Dimonstein, G. *Children Dance in the Classroom.* New York: Macmillan, 1971.

Duncan, Irma. *The Technique of Isadora Duncan.* New York: Kamin, no date.

Duncan, Isadora. *The Art of Dance.* Edited by S. Cheney. New York: Theatre Arts, 1928.

Feldenkrais, M. *Awareness through Movement: Health Exercises for Personal Growth.* New York: Harper & Row, 1972.

Feldenkrais, M. *Body and Mature Behavior.* New York: International Universities Press, 1970.

Freedman, M. B., and Sweet, B. S. "Some Specific Features of Group Psychotherapy and Their Implications for Selected Patients." *International Journal of Group Psychotherapy* 4 (1954), pp. 355-68.

Hanh, T. N. *The Miracle of Mindfulness! A Manual on Meditation.* Boston: Beacon Press, 1976.

Harwood, A. C. *The Recovery of Man in Childhood: A Study in the Educational Work of Rudolf Steiner.* Spring Valley, N.Y.: Anthroposophic Press, 1958.

Krystal, H. "Alexithymia and Psychotherapy." *American Journal of Psychotherapy* 33 (1979), pp. 17-31.

Lynch, J. J. *The Language of the Heart: The Human Body in Dialogue.* New York: Basic Books, 1985.

Martin, J. "Isadora and Basic Dance." In *Isadora Duncan,* edited by P. Magriel. New York: Henry Holt, 1947.

Marty, P., and de M'Usan, M. "La pensée operatoire." *Révue François Psychoanalysis* 27 (supplement 1963), p. 1345.

Masters, R., and Houston, J. *Listening to the Body: The Psychophysical Way to Health and Awareness.* New York: Dell/Delta, 1978.

Needleman, J. *A Sense of the Cosmos.* New York: Doubleday, 1975.

Penfield, W. *The Mystery of the Mind: A Critical Study of Consciousness and the Human Brain.* Princeton: Princeton University Press, 1975.

Richards, M. C. *Toward Wholeness: Rudolf Steiner Education in America.* Middletown, Conn.: Wesleyan University Press, 1980.

Shelton, H. M. *Exercise!* Chicago: Natural Hygiene Press, 1971.

Sifneos, P. E. "Problems of Psychotherapy of Patients with Alexithymic Characteristics and Physical Disease." *Psychotherapeutics and Psychosomatics* 26 (1975), p. 68.

Steiner, R. *Education of the Child in the Light of Anthroposophy.* Translated by G. Adams. and M. Adams. London: Rudolf Steiner Press, 1976.

Tobias, Tobi. *New York Times,* 22 May 1977.

7

Subject Connections

Subjects have been traditionally at the centre of schooling. In the transmission curriculum they become central as subject matter can be taught in a manner unrelated to the needs and interests of students. In the holistic curriculum we attempt to make a number of connections with subject matter. One of the most important is between self and subject. If we can relate subject matter to the inner life of the child, subjects become less abstract and irrelevant. It is also important to explore connections between subjects; this can be done through various integrated approaches to curriculum as well as through holistic thinking models. Finally, subjects can connect the self to society. In this chapter we explore all of these connections.

Self/Subject

We have already touched on self and subject matter in chapter 5 when we looked at visualization. Some of the guided imagery exercises can motivate student interest as well as develop student understanding. Perhaps one of the best examples of connecting self and subject comes from the work of Sylvia Ashton-Warner in her book *Teacher*. Ashton-Warner (1963) acknowledges that her approach is not new as she cites the work of Tolstoy and Anne Sullivan, the teacher of Helen Keller. For Ashton-Warner, organic reading is "the bridge from the known to the unknown; from the native culture to a new; and universally speaking, from the inner man out" (p. 26).

Ashton-Warner characterizes children as having two visions, an inner and outer, and she believes the inner is more powerful and must be reached if learning is to occur. Ashton-Warner reached this inner vision through what she calls "key vocabulary." These are words that have intense meaning to children and are "already part of the dynamic life" (p. 32). Key vocabulary for the Maori children consisted of such words as "Mummy", "Daddy", "kiss", "frightened", and "ghost," which Ashton-Warner wrote down on cards for each child. Each student would then develop their own set of key words and Ashton-Warner would have the student read the cards back to her. The children also would read their words to other students in pairs; by doing this the students would quickly develop basic reading skills.

After the student has developed about forty words in the key vocabulary, Ashton-Warner moved to organic writing. She says, "Whereas the Key Vocabulary is a one-word caption of the inner world, creative writing is a sentence-length or story-length caption'' (p. 47). These sentences and stories are usually autobiographical. For Ashton-Warner the writing, spelling, and composition emerge holistically. She states: ''spelling and composition are no longer separate subjects to be taught but emerge naturally as another medium'' (p. 49). Drawings are combined with the stories to form what Ashton-Warner calls the ''most dramatic and pathetic and colourful things I've ever seen on pages'' (p. 49).

The ideas for the stories always come from the students as she does not give them something to write about; she calls that an imposition.

> I never teach a child something and then get him to write about it. It would be an imposition in the way that it is in art. A child's writing is his own affair and is an exercise in integration which makes for better work. The more it means to him the more value it is to him. And it means everything to him. It is part of him as an arranged subject could never be. It is not a page of sentences written round set words, resulting in a jumble of disconnected facts as you so often see. It is the unbroken line of thought that we cultivate so carefully in our own writing and conversation. (pp. 49-50)

Ashton-Warner taught the Maori children math in the same organic way. For her, nature and number are intimately linked so that she would take the children outside. She taught them about the Golden Section, which is the ideal proportion in nature and is ''the division of a distance in such a way that the shorter part is to the longer part as the longer part is to the whole'' (p. 68). Ashton-Warner states that fern fronds make wonderful things for young children to count. The Golden Section ''becomes inseparable from writing and reading and drawing and conversation. Three ducks on the wing we like better than three ducks on a number card with a static three beside them'' (p. 70).

Ashton-Warner's approach to subject matter is to start with the inner vision of the child and build on it. The inner vision becomes the key vocabulary, which in turn forms the basis for writing and reading. Her pedagogy, then, is rooted in the inner person and is connected to nature. As much as possible, she avoids artificial impositions on the child's inner vision.

Ashton-Warner (1963) quotes C. E. Beeby at the beginning of her chapter on Organic Writing, and it is worth citing here as a conclusion to this section because it sums up her holistic approach so well. ''Life as a whole is too complicated to teach to children. The minute it is cut up they can understand it, but you are liable to kill it in cutting it up'' (p. 46).

Subject/Subject Connections

Waldorf Education/Main lesson. In the Waldorf school the morning's instruction begins with the main lesson. The main lesson runs from approximately 9:00 to 11:00 a.m. In Waldorf education the same teacher stays with the children from grades 1 to 8 and one of their main responsibilities each day is the main lesson.

The main lesson incorporates English, mathematics, geography, history, and science. The main vehicle for integration is the artistic sense of the teacher. The lesson can often start with singing or a speech chorus of poems that the students are learning.

Steiner recognized that young children love ritual and it is built into many aspects of the program. The singing might be followed by teacher presentation on the main theme.

Central to each main lesson are the arts, as it is the artistic sense that integrates the main lesson. Each student has an unlined notebook where they draw in color what they are learning. According to Richards (1980):

> Each Main Lesson will call upon the child's powers of listening, of body movement, of thinking, and of feeling. Artistic activity is particularly related to the will: it is an experience of doing, of making. Artwork also invites the child's feeling for expressiveness and encourages a kind of intuitive thinking about how to get things done. In the early grades, some teachers allow the children to copy what has been drawn on the board so that they may learn to draw in ways they would not otherwise know. Other times the children draw freely. Variety exists, according to teacher and grade. (p. 25)

Wax crayons and colored pencils are used as well as water colors. The student is encouraged to feel the color as he or she draws so that the artistic experience is not abstract. In the early grades the coloring can follow the telling of a story so that language is connected to art. The student may mix primary colors such as yellow and blue to make green. Again a story is often told before the mixing of the colors so the experience is connected to the child's imagination. Black and white are not usually mixed at the lower grades because they are more abstract and not as dynamic for the younger child. Similarly, the children do not draw outline shapes but fill in shapes with color. Shapes tend to come from the color rather than from hard boundaries. Art is also connected to math as painting, modelling, designing, and string constructions are used (Richards, 1980, p. 26).

Storytelling can be used in teaching science; for example, Wilkinson (1975) suggests that the following story can be used to teach young children about the four elements:

> Once upon a time there was a big brown seed, with white edges and white stripes, which was lying on the ground. The gnomes who lived in that part of the garden knew that it was a seed and that they ought to look after it, so they quietly buried it. Then they told the water fairies about it and the water fairies came down in the rain to give it something to drink. Soon the fire fairies who live in the sun's warmth came on a visit and the seed began to feel strange, as if some change were taking place. It seemed to be getting bigger and soon its jacket burst. One shoot went downwards into the earth and another shoot came up out of the ground. The little shoot that went downwards grew into a root and all the springtime the gnomes were busy looking after it and the soil around it. The rain and the fire fairies kept visiting the growing plant, and the air fairies also came and danced around it. For months it grew, taller than you, and as tall as I am, and then, at the top of the stalk something quite wonderful happened. A huge yellow flower appeared turning its face towards the sun. Some children came to look at it and they said, "What a big shining face, just like the sun. We will call it a sunflower." (p. 72)

In grade 5, one teacher made the following connection between botany, music, and poetry:

As an introduction to our study of the plant kingdom, I led the children from a dramatic story of the seed's awakening to their own creative expressions of this birth of life forces. Each child discovered a tonal harmony which we then moved to by using our cupped hands to be the seed. Then as the melody was played, our hands followed the opening of the seed, roots' first search, uplifting of the seed-enclosed seed leaves, breaking into light and warmth, spreading of the seed leaves, upward striving of the stem and then — the first true leaves. All this formed by a few notes! A poem-like expression followed. (Richards, 1980, p. 114)

The students wrote a tune which they then played on the recorder and then wrote a poem. Richards (1980) argues that through art, Waldorf education attempts to develop an intuitive seeing which is missing in our culture:

It is an intuitive seeing, which comes about as a result of exercising and experiencing one's physical senses imaginatively, wholeheartedly, and wholesoulfully. This is why artistic practice is so important in all learning and education. This is why neglect of the artist in each person is so impoverishing to society. Without this spiritual sense organ, this way of seeing the formative forces at work in a physical process, we are blind and duped by appearances. (p. 73)

Steiner encouraged teachers to be creative and flexible in their approach. According to Richards (1980), they "paint and draw, sing and play recorder, recite and tell stories, and cook and play with the children" (p. 28). Steiner wanted the teacher to appeal to the interests of the child and also to use humor and surprise in the classroom. He wanted the teachers to teach from enthusiasm rather than a rigid schedule. Steiner (1976) said to teachers at the first Waldorf school before it opened:

The teacher must be a person of initiative in everything that he does, great and small. . . .

The teacher should be one who is interested in the being of the whole world and of humanity. . . .

The teacher must be one who never makes a compromise in his heart and mind with what is untrue. . . .

The teacher must never get stale or grow sour. . . .

During this fortnight I have only spoken of what can enter directly into your practical teaching, if you allow it first to work rightly within your own souls. But our Waldorf School, my dear friends, will depend upon what you do within yourselves, and whether you really allow the things which we have been considering to become effective in your own souls. . . .

I do not want to make you into teaching machines, but into free independent teachers. . . .

Let us in particular keep before us this thought which shall truly fill our hearts and minds: That bound up with the spiritual movement of the present day are also the spiritual powers that guide the Universe. If we believe in these good spiritual powers, then they will be the inspirers of our lives and we shall really be enabled to teach. (pp. 199-201)

Holistic Thinking. While Waldorf uses art as integrator of subject matter, it is possible to use thinking models as vehicles for making connections across subjects (Ross and Maynes, 1982). I believe it is also possible to use holistic thinking, which links linear thinking and intuition in the same manner. Some creative thinking models, such as the model developed by Osborn (1953) and Parnes (1981), move in this direction. Alex Osborn emphasized such principles as deferred judgment which separates generating ideas from evaluating ideas. To generate ideas Osborn developed the concept of brainstorming where the person or group develops as many ideas as possible without immediate evaluation. Once the brainstorming is completed evaluation and synthesis of the ideas can begin.

Parnes was responsible for taking the principles of Osborn and building a creative problem-solving (CPS) model. The model consists of five steps:

1. Fact Finding
2. Problem Finding
3. Idea Finding
4. Solution Finding
5. Acceptance Finding

Isaken and Treffinger (1985) have revised this model somewhat and have develop a six-step approach:

— Mess Finding
— Data Finding
— Problem Finding
— Idea Finding
— Solution Finding
— Acceptance Finding

The process is outlined in Figure 3 on page 105.

I would also like to propose an approach based on extension of the Wallas model described in chapter 5. The steps to the model include:

— Uncertainty/Ambiguity
— Problem Clarification
— Preparation/Frameworking
— Incubation
— Alternative Search
— Illumination/Alternative selection
— Verification

Uncertainty/Ambiguity. Most problem-solving is prodded by an unresolved situation. For example, in writing this book the lack of clarity about holistic education was a factor that encouraged me to explore this area in more depth. I had done some exploration in a course I teach entitled ''The Holistic Curriculum,'' but there remained a great deal of ambiguity in my mind about both the context and practice

Figure 3/Creative Problem-Solving Process

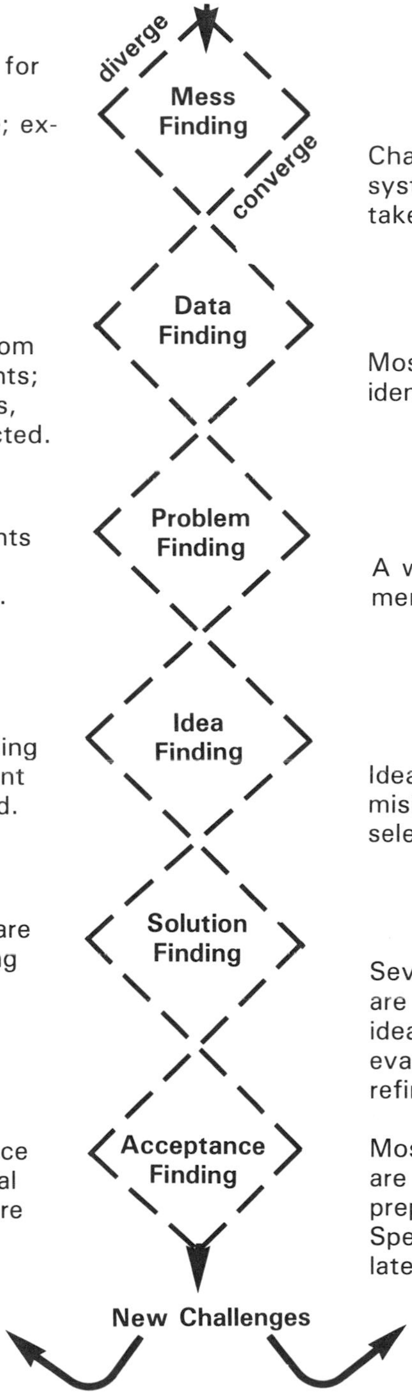

Divergent Phase | **Problem Sensitivity** | **Convergent Phase**

Experiences, roles and situations are searched for messes . . .
openness to experience; exploring opportunities.

diverge

Mess Finding

converge

Challenge is accepted and systematic efforts undertaken to respond to it.

Data are gathered; the situation is examined from many different viewpoints; information, impressions, feelings, etc., are collected.

Data Finding

Most important data are identified and analysed.

Many possible statements of problems and sub-problems are generated.

Problem Finding

A working problem statement is chosen.

Many alternatives and possibilities for responding to the problem statement are developed and listed.

Idea Finding

Ideas that seem most promising or interesting are selected.

Many possible criteria are formulated for reviewing and evaluating ideas.

Solution Finding

Several important criteria are selected to evaluate ideas. Criteria are used to evaluate, strengthen, and refine ideas.

Possible sources of assistance and resistance are considered; potential implementation steps are identified.

Acceptance Finding

Most promising solutions are focussed on and prepared for action; Specific plans are formulated to implement solution.

New Challenges

105

of the holistic curriculum. In a sense, this book was a chance to explore holistic education in a more complete way.

Problem Clarification. In this step the person or group attempts to get some sort of handle on the problem. This might be done by writing out a problem statement. Unlike logical mathematical problem-solving, the problem statement is not a hypothesis in the technical sense; instead, it attempts to get at the root of the problem. Imagery and intuition can be used at this stage to help sort out the problem; by inner reflection the central issue may come forth. In writing this book, problem clarification involved settling on the definition presented in the Introduction. I had been working with this definition for two years in discussions with my students, although I reworked it again for this book. The definition has provided an initial framework for the book.

Preparation/Frameworking. Here one attempts to develop a more complete framework for the problem as one tries to see the problem from a broader perspective than in the previous step. For the book, this involved developing an outline in the form of chapter headings that was also congruent with the definition. This step tends to involve more linear thinking as each aspect of the framework is explored; however, imagery and intuition can still be at play here. It is possible, for example, for one to have an image of either part of the framework or a vision of the entire approach.

Incubation. Incubation can occur throughout the problem-solving process. In fact, although these steps are presented in a linear order, the approach I am describing is really much more fluid and is not a step-by-step process. In Beeby's words I risk killing the whole thing by breaking it into parts.

Incubation involves a standing back and letting the elements work themselves through at a subconscious level. If we force the problem-solving process too much, then it will be much less productive. In working on this book, as well as others I have written, I often find ideas popping into my head while meditating, walking, driving, or taking a bath.

Alternative Search. This usually involves a more conscious search for alternatives as well as an examination of the alternatives. Alternative courses of action are first explored and developed, and then judged against criteria. These criteria can be developed consciously and can include a number of factors, or only a few which are felt more intuitively. Ultimately, these criteria are usually related to the framework. It is also possible that examining alternatives can change the original framework. Again, this whole problem-solving process tends to go back-and-forth rather than progress in a logical sequence. For example, I reworked the original definition of holistic education after I began the second half of this book.

With this book I have also attempted to link ideas for each chapter to the overall conception of holistic education. For example, with regard to metaphor, I had to consider whether this topic was congruent with the overall conception and whether it would also stimulate teacher interest? Are the examples of metaphor in the classroom adequate, or should I look for others?

Alternative Selection/Illumination. Here the person settles on a course of action. This can involve a rational assessment of the alternatives against the criteria, or it may involve the appearance of an image as outlined in chapter 5. If an image or intuitive insight does occur, it can also be assessed against the criteria, but we have to be careful that our criteria and mind-set do not become too rigid. If the criteria are too inflexible, creativity will be stifled. If the vision is a powerful one, the criteria themselves may have to be reworked.

Verification. Now the solution must be tested. In short, does it work or must you search for other solutions? With regard to this book, it must be reviewed. The reviewers may recommend alternatives which can range from reworking small sections of the text, to reorganizing and rewriting a large amount of material. The reviewers are an important first step in verification of the book. A second step in the verification comes from the type of readership the book attracts.

This model can also be applied to problems and projects that the student confronts in different subjects. For example, students could look at the issue of whether the Meech Lake accord revising the Canadian Constitution should have been signed.

Ambiguity/Uncertainty. Uncertainty involves leaving Quebec out of the constitutional agreement signed in 1982. The Meech Lake accord brings Quebec into the constitution, but some critics (for example, Trudeau) feel that it reduces federal power too much.

Problem Clarification. Should the Meech Lake accord be signed?

Preparation/Frameworking. This step involves looking closely at the provisions of the accord and at one's vision of Canada. The students can first develop their own vision of Canada. For example, do they see the country run by a strong central government which can determine the course of action regarding issues such as control of oil reserves or the administration of health care systems. Or alternatively, do they see Canada as more decentralized where the provinces have a strong say in these issues. Students could in fact do some visualization about how they see Canada and also how they see various ethnic groups as part of the social fabric. After working through their own vision they can look closely at the provisions in the Meech Lake accord so that they understand what was proposed.

Incubation. Let the students step back from the problem for awhile. They can discuss the issues involved, but it can be helpful just to let things sit for awhile (for example, a few days) as they let their sense of Canada develop along with the relation of the accord to their vision.

Alternative Search. Here the students deal with the issue more consciously as they develop their vision more clearly and compare it with the accord. In what ways does the accord match their vision and in what ways does it not? The students approach this systematically by writing out their vision and listing the provisions that they agree with and those that they disagree with. Their vision becomes the criteria for assessing the accord.

Alternative Selection/Illumination. The students decide whether they would actually sign the accord. After the more systematic alternative search, the students can step back again and do some more reflection (for example, a short meditation) on the decision. After the inner reflection, there is a greater chance that the decision will not be an abstract one but one more connected to the whole person. Students can then write down their decision and the reasons for it.

Verification. In this last step the students can share their answers with other students and the teacher. They can also compare it to other responses to the accord.

There are many problem-solving processes that are available to teachers which can allow for subject connections. By employing these models in different disciplines we can explore connections between the subjects. My purpose in presenting the above approach is to explore approaches to problem-solving that are less linear and allow for intuition, incubation, and imagery.

Subjects and Values. A third way of exploring connections between subjects is through values. All subjects have a value dimension, although this dimension is more apparent in some subjects (for example, language and social studies) than in others (for example, mathematics). As noted in chapter 1, the holistic curriculum acknowledges our lives to be infused with moral and value conflicts and that these should not be ignored in the curriculum. By recognizing that each subject can be approached through values, another unifying thread in the curriculum is provided. Harmin, Kirschenbaum, and Simon (1973) have argued that each subject has three levels — facts, concepts, and values. Although somewhat simplistic, this model is helpful at an initial stage in exploring values in different subject areas.

It is also possible to focus on key issues that are permeated with values. A current issue is AIDS and it allows for interdisciplinary inquiry based on values questions. For example, students could examine the scientific side of the issue by learning about the AIDS viruses and the current efforts to treat patients with drugs such as AZT. At the same time, there are ethical questions about how AIDS patients are treated by some health professionals. In some cases patients have been isolated and shunned. Why has the health care profession done this, and is it right? The students could also look at the social and psychological side of AIDS, again keeping the values dimension as a link in the whole process. For example, they could look at how AIDS patients have been treated by society and why some people have tried to hide AIDS as the cause of death. The coroner's intervention following the death of the American entertainer Liberace could be discussed. Was it right for the coroner to intervene and make the cause of death public? Does the person have a right to privacy concerning the cause of death? Elizabeth Kubler-Ross tried to set up a home for AIDS children, but the community in which she lives objected so she gave up. What are the issues involved in this case?

Values can be a useful link, particularly if the teacher is taking a problem-centred approach to learning. In this way values questions can be integrated into the problems presented to the student.

Subject/Community

Subjects can also provide a bridge to community. This topic will also be explored in the next chapter, but it is important to provide at least one example here. The example I have chosen is The Foxfire project, conducted under the leadership of Elliot Wigginton (1986). Wigginton began by teaching English at Rabun Gap-Nacochee school in the southern Appalachian Mountains. In order to get his students involved in the writing–editing process he started a magazine in 1966 called *Foxfire*. The first issue was edited by grade 10 students under Wigginton's general leadership. The magazine became very popular because of the interviews with people in the surrounding community. For example, senior citizens were interviewed and provided practical advice on such matters as how to find and use yellowroot, a herbal medicine; how to make a cotton hamper; and how to weave handspun wool into cloth. Some of the contacts with people in the community became so frequent that individuals like Aunt Arie, who lived alone in a log house on a mountainside, became a permanent part of the students' lives. Students visited her frequently to watch her planting and cooking, and she in turn would frequently visit Wigginton's classroom.

One of the most ambitious projects was devoted on how to build a log cabin. This issue led to a literary award from the Georgia Writers' Association. Eventually, the readership for *Foxfire* became so large that it led to several books by the same name. Ten years after the first *Foxfire* book was published, a celebration was held in conjunction with the release of *Foxfire 7*. The celebration took place in conjunction with the annual Mother's Day picnic which is held each year by the *Foxfire* staff to honor people in the community who have been involved in the magazine. Contact between the students and community even spreads into other areas as students help some of the senior citizens with chores around their home (for example, painting). *Foxfire* is still published today and is part of the curriculum in the public school in Ruban Gap. Students work in all areas connected with the production of the magazine, from running an archive of tapes to speaking to other schools and groups around the United States. The students even assisted in the development of a script for the Broadway hit *Foxfire*. There is also now a videotape and television component of Foxfire which shows productions on the local cable network. Again the central focus is on interviewing local residents about local customs and issues that they face in their lives.

Foxfire also started its own publishing company, Foxfire Press, whose products are distributed by E. P. Dutton. The publishing division is housed in a passive solar building. The first publication from the press was *Aunt Arie: Foxfire Portrait*.

Foxfire is much more than a success story. It is about how one teacher trusted his students and allowed them to go out into the surrounding community to interview people and use those interviews to develop a publication. This publication became a vehicle for teaching students language skills as well as the means for connecting language to the community.

In his recent book, Wigginton (1986) lists what he calls "some overarching truths" about teaching. The first truth is "fine teachers see their subject matter whole." Wigginton states that teachers "are their subject matter, and for them, the inescapable linkages between that subject matter, their communities, their students, and the globe come so automatically that for them to teach otherwise — to teach a course in isolation from the world outside the school facility — would be impossible" (p. 200).

He then lists some questions which show how inquiry can connect the student to the community.

> The first spring flowers become targets of botanical scrutiny. And never in isolation, for each step inevitably leads to the next: Why do those spring flowers have color and fragrance? How do they acquire it? Of what is it made? What is the connection between flowers and bees? How do bees work? How do they communicate? How do they build? Why are the cells in their combs hexagonal? Are there relationships between their architecture and Buckminster Fuller's domes? What is the mathematics involved? What materials are strongest? Why do people write poems about flowers? What have they written? Why do they give flowers to each other? Do the colors of the flowers they give mean anything? Why? Why do some plant species become endangered? How can we stop that? Why should we? What do environmental scientists do? What do landscape architects do? Why? (pp. 200-201)

Confluent Education

I would like to close this chapter with a brief discussion on confluent education. Confluent education has developed a number of strategies to facilitate connections between self–subject, subject–subject, and subject–community. Confluent education was begun in the 1960s under the leadership of George Brown and was initially concerned with connecting the cognitive and affective domains. In the 1970s, however, the focus became broader as confluent education was seen to deal with the intrapersonal, interpersonal, extrapersonal, and transpersonal (Brown, Phillips and Shapiro, 1976). The four dimensions are presented as concentric circles:

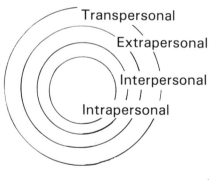

(p. 10)

The intrapersonal refers to the person's internal feelings and self-perceptions. The intrapersonal also refers to a person's subpersonalities such as aggressive or passive, masculine and feminine, as well as other subselves. Confluent education attempts to facilitate awareness of the subselves and helps the student bring them into harmony.

The interpersonal dimension consists of relations with others, how students perceive other people, and how they communicate with them. The third dimension, the extrapersonal, refers to the context or social structures that encompass the experiences of the student. These include the structure of the school, the community, and society. Brown, Phillips, and Shapiro (1976) argue that the three dimensions are interrelated and that the most desirable state is where all three are integrated.

> For example, if a curriculum is designed to teach democratic processes, and individual students share in decisions affecting them, work in small groups in a decision-making process, and participate with the teacher in setting classroom rules, a confluence exists among intrapersonal needs, interpersonal relations, and the extrapersonal setting. If the teacher governs the class autocratically, however, the situation is not confluent. (pp. 11-12)

The fourth dimension, the transpersonal, surrounds the first three and refers to the cosmic or spiritual dimension of the student's experience. The transpersonal provides the universal context for examining basic questions of meaning and spirituality.

Below are some examples of confluent education exploring the various subject connections.

Self-Subject. This example by Jean Schleifer (1975) concentrates on how the student can make connections with a novel they have been reading, particularly a character who was important to the student.

1. Close your eyes. Get into your own private space. Now — from the book you read, try to see the person who means the most to you. Put the person somewhere, either in a place he would naturally be according to the book or a place where you can imagine his being. Try to see every part of the person. What does the hair look like? What color? Length? Curly? Straight? Windblown? Neat? Notice the ears. What kind of nose? Notice the skin. Clear, pimply, tanned? How do you see the mouth? Full? Drooped? Clenched? What is the person doing with the hands? How does the person stand? Walk? What kind of clothes? See them distinctly — the colors, the style, etc.
2. When you are ready, open your eyes. Write a description of your person's appearance.
3. Choose one word from what you have written that is the essence of the description of the person. Write it down.
4. Now write down what to you would be an opposite word — one word.
5. Tell your words. Talk about them.
6. Turn your paper over. Draw, in lines or colors, the way you see the person. Don't try to draw a photographic picture. Show the person through shapes, colors, and lines. Talk to others. (p. 252)

This exercise also asks the student to use art (drawing), so it also makes subject–subject connections.

Subject–Subject. The following activity is for the elementary school from Gloria Castillo (1978) and makes connections between science, language, drama, and movement.

111

Be the sun. Talk as if you are the sun. Example: "I am the sun. I am a very large star. I have a great deal of heat. My heat gives energy to the earth."

Now, be the earth. Talk as if you are the earth. Example: "I am the earth. I have air, water, plants, and animals."

One person be the sun and another be the earth. Create a conversation between the sun and the earth. What do you have to say to one another?

Let this be an activity in improvisational theatre as well as in science. Do not correct the students if they should offer incorrect statements. After the "play", you can clarify points, give additional information, or assign further readings. Use this activity to assess what the students do and do not know about the sun and the earth.

With advanced students, add other planets of our solar system to the "play."

Dance around as if you are the earth. Circle the room once to represent one day. Choose a partner. One be the earth, the other the moon. Earth and moon dance together, in time to one another. Now both join another partnership. Two of you become the sun. All of you dance together as if you are the sun (two students), moon, and earth dancing together.

Depending on the ability of the class to do this, continue to add students to represent other solar bodies. Create a solar system dance. (pp. 194-95)

Subject–Community. Sandra Newby (1975) developed a program for her grade 9 English class that included a community component. She encouraged her students to organize a newspaper, record interviews, and produce videotapes based on contact with someone outside the school.

References

Ashton-Warner, Sylvia. *Teacher.* New York: Bantam, 1964.

Brown, G. I.; Phillips, M.; and Shapiro, S. *Getting It All Together: Confluent Education.* Bloomington, Indiana: Phi Delta Kappa Educational Foundation, 1976.

Castillo, Gloria. *Left Handed Teaching: Lessons in Affective Education.* New York: Holt Rinehart & Winston, 1978.

Harmin, M.; Kirschenbaum, H.; and Simon, S. B. *Clarifying Values through Subject Matter: Applications for the Classroom.* Minneapolis: Winston Press, 1973.

Harwood, A. C. *The Recovery of Man in Childhood: A Study in the Educational Work of Rudolf Steiner.* Spring Valley, N.Y.: Anthroposophic Press, 1958.

Isaksen, S. G., and Treffinger, D. J. *Creative Problem Solving: The Basic Course.* Buffalo, N.Y.: Bearly Limited, 1985.

Newby, S. ''Getting a Responsibility in a Ninth-Grade English Class.'' In *The Live Classroom: Innovation through Confluent Education and Gestalt,* edited by G. I. Brown. New York: Viking, 1975.

Osborn, A. F. *Applied Imagination.* New York: Scribners, 1953.

Parnes, S. J. *The Magic of Your Mind.* Buffalo, N.Y.: Bearly Limited, 1981.

Richards, M. V. *Toward Wholeness: Rudolf Steiner Education in America.* Middletown, Conn.: Wesleyan University Press, 1980.

Ross, J. A., and Maynes, F. *Teaching Problem Solving.* Toronto: Ontario Institute for Studies in Education, 1982.

Schleifer, J. ''Listening to the Book.'' In *The Live Classroom: Innovation through Confluent Education and Gestalt,* edited by G. E. Brown. New York: Viking, 1975.

8

Community Connections

The holistic curriculum should foster connections between student and community. The most immediate community for the student is the classroom, and co-operative education with its emphasis on learning teams attempts to foster community within classrooms. A somewhat larger community is the school, and both invitational education and social literacy training attempt to facilitate community within the school. Finally, there are programs which attempt to connect the student to the larger community that surrounds the school. These programs often involve the student in community service activities or in social change programs.

Self–Classroom Connections

Control Theory/Co-operative Learning. William Glasser (1986) has long been an advocate of making the classroom a community. In one of his earlier books Glasser (1969) argued for the classroom meeting as a vehicle to enhance student self-esteem as well as to help develop a sense of community in the classroom. In the classroom meeting students attempt to solve problems in a large group setting.

Most recently, Glasser has argued for control theory, which is based on the assumption that human behavior is generated by what goes on inside the person. According to control theory, we can't really force kids to do things in the classroom; instead we only attempt to provide an environment that meets their needs. Control theory suggests there are five basic needs: "(1) to survive and reproduce . . . (2) to belong and love, (3) to gain power, (4) to be free and (5) to have fun" (p. 24).

It is the need to gain power that is central to control theory. If students don't feel that what they are doing in school is of any importance, they simply won't learn. Glasser feels that the need for power is at the core of almost all school problems. According to Glasser, most approaches to school disciplines ignore control theory and attempt to influence student behavior by external stimuli. On the other hand, teachers who rarely have discipline problems develop a classroom environment where the student feels accepted and has the sense that what he or she is doing in the classroom is important. Glasser (1987) notes that the "band teacher, the chorus teacher, the drama teacher, or the football coach" rarely "have problems with students not working, not paying attention, and not behaving'' (p. 658). These teachers tend not to have problems because they meet the students need for belonging and power.

Glasser is an advocate of using learning teams in classrooms. In most classrooms Glasser (1987) claims ''each student works alone. He or she is told, 'Keep your eyes on your own work; don't share; don't compare; don't talk; don't help' '' (p. 659). Of course, this is contrary to the basic human need to belong. In contrast, the learning team usually involves four or five students working together to achieve a group goal. Often the group will consist of one high achieving student, a low achieving student, and two or three average students. Glasser (1987) draws an analogy to a basketball team to make his point about how each member of the team can feel valuable even though each person is making a different type of contribution:

> One basketball player may average 30 points per game and another player may average only two points per game, but the first player is not necessarily considered better than the second. The player who scores only two points may feed the ball to the player who scores 30 points; without his or her accurate passes, the high scorer would be helpless. The coach doesn't give the high scorer a better grade than the low scorer. Since the team's grade is the final score, which members of the team earn together, the coach tries to teach them to cooperate, to talk to each other on the floor, to pass the ball off, to make each game as much a team effort as possible. (p. 660)

Activities that learning teams can pursue include writing a skit, discussing a book, writing a paper, and doing a research project. Glasser has found that students can develop the same sense of group loyalty on a learning team as they do on an athletic team. In fact, he claims that the former low achiever is hard to recognize in a learning team because he or she often is more productive in the group context.

The learning team concept is based, in part, on the work of David Johnson and Roger Johnson (1986) at the University of Minnesota. The Johnsons have promoted the concept of co-operative learning. Roy Smith (1987), who uses co-operative learning in his classroom, has discussed how he develops co-operative skills in his classroom.

First, the teacher should tell their students that co-operative learning is a priority and encourage sharing of materials and the development of communication skills. Smith claims the teacher often will downplay co-operation. For example, he (1987) says: ''I heard one teacher tell a class that had just completed a cooperative brainstorming session, 'Okay, let's get back to work.' The implication was that group work is entertaining but that real work begins when the students return to individual activities at their own desks'' (p. 664).

Second, the teacher should work on the necessary skills to develop co-operation by concentrating on one or two skills at a time. For example, the teacher might focus on listening as a skill for two or three classroom sessions because it is so fundamental to co-operative learning. The teacher will also want to keep in close contact with the learning teams to see which skills are needed. The teacher may want the students to take the following roles in groups because they are helpful in facilitating the group achieve its task.

1. ENCOURAGER of PARTICIPATION. In a friendly way encourages all

members of the group to participate in the discussion, sharing their ideas
and feelings.
2. PRAISER. Compliments group members who do their assigned work and
    contribute to the learning of the group.
3. SUMMARIZER. Restates the ideas and feelings expressed in the discussion
    whenever it is appropriate.
4. CHECKER. Makes sure everyone has read and edited two compositions and
    that everyone understands the general principles of writing thesis essays.

(Glasser, 1986, p. 100)

The teacher can introduce these roles to the whole class and then set up the learning teams with each member taking one of these roles. After they have dealt with
these skills in this direct manner, they can then integrate them into their group behavior.

After working with the specific skills, the third step involves the teacher working
with the students to help them practice the skills in different situations. For example,
some students can act as observers of the learning teams and record how they listen,
encourage, praise, summarize, and check. After the observation, the students can
share their feedback with the learning teams.

Feedback is the fourth step in developing co-operative learning. In addition to
observers providing feedback, group members also can supply feedback to each other
after the session is finished. Some teachers furnish check lists with the social skills
listed to help students in this task. It is important that students concentrate on specifics
in giving feedback so that the person can deal with the information in a constructive
way. Smith says, ''It is important that observers avoid statements that evaluate, such
as 'Amy did a good job.' Instead, an observer should report, 'I saw Amy ask others
for their opinions four times' '' (p. 665).

The fifth and final step involves persevering in using co-operative skills. The teacher
needs to keep these skills in the forefront and not let them take a backseat to academic
work. Co-operative skills and academic work should work together to facilitate student intellectual, emotional, and social growth.

Smith has used learning teams in language study and history. For example, he has
used groups of three to study vocabulary. Each group consists of one member from
the top third of the class, the middle third, and the bottom third. The groupings are
based on a pretest given by Smith. Each member looks up words independently and
then they come together to discuss the meaning of the words they have looked up.
After discussing the words, the students take two quizzes; the first is a group quiz
that the team works on co-operatively; the second is an individual quiz, since Smith
feels individual accountability is also important.

Another task involves groups of four researching aspects of medieval life and then
presenting their findings in the form of a newspaper. Each team can focus on one
aspect of medieval life so the paper deals with one theme or individual. This theme
is developed in the paper with news stories, editorials, feature items, as well as car-
toons, advertisements, and obituaries. Each group member has ''two distinct tasks:
1) to do the best possible work on his or her writing assignment, and 2) to help other
group members by reading their articles and checking the facts, the sentence structure, the spelling, the punctuation, the coherence, the development of the topic, and
the unity'' (p. 666).

Smith asked his grade 9 class to discuss the advantages and disadvantages of team learning. Some of the disadvantages included interpersonal problems that developed in some teams, poor listening by some students, and the fact that some students don't do their share of the work. Students found the advantages included exposure to more ideas, improved performance for some students, developing responsibility through commitment to the group effort and enjoying learning more. I have used learning teams for years in my graduate courses and have found many of the same advantages listed by Smith's students.

Self–School Connections

Invitational Education/The Inviting School. William Purkey and John Novak (1984) have developed what they call an invitational approach to education. They define invitational education literally as "the process by which people are cordially summoned to realize their relatively boundless potential" (p. 3). There are four levels to invitational education. The first level is being intentionally disinviting. At this level the teacher or principal makes statements that are deliberately disinviting such as "You never use your head" and "Why can't you do as well as your brother." The second level is called unintentionally disinviting and involves statements or gestures that are well-intentioned but are disinviting to the students. A statement such as "It's easy, anyone can do it" is at this level, because it makes the student feel inadequate, particularly if he or she has been trying very hard to do the assigned task. Below are some disinviting comments and behaviors:

Disinviting Comments	*Disinviting Behaviors*
Keep out.	Giving a thumbs-down sign
What May is trying to say is. . .	Interrupting
Use your head.	Looking at your watch
It won't work.	Yawning in someone's face
You'll have to call back.	Shaking your finger at someone
You can't do that.	Scowling and frowning
I don't care what you do.	Slamming a door
Not bad, for a girl.	Using ridicule
Don't be so stupid.	Turning your back on someone
Who do you think you are?	Cutting people short
He can't be disturbed.	Making fun of a person
Why didn't you stay at home?	Looking away from someone
Woman driver.	Leaving someone to answer the
They don't want to learn.	phone
They don't have the ability.	Hitting someone
You can't be that dumb.	Being obscene
You ought to know better.	Laughing at someone's misfortune

(pp. 132-33)

Level three is unintentionally inviting and consists of behaviors that have a positive effect on students, although the teacher usually cannot explain why they taught or acted in that way. According to Purkey and Novak, people functioning at this level can sometimes become confused and disoriented and revert to disinviting behavior because they have not developed their approach in a consistent way. The fourth and final level is being intentionally inviting. Here, educators through sustained effort have integrated inviting behavior into their life so that they "work with" the students rather than "doing things to" the students. The following are some inviting comments and behaviors:

Inviting Behaviors	*Inviting Comments*
A relaxed posture	Good morning.
Lending a book	Thanks very much.
Smiling	Congratulations.
Listening carefully	Let's talk it over.
Patting a back	How can I help?
Shaking hands	I appreciate your help.
Opening a door for someone	Happy birthday!
Giving a friendly wink	I enjoy having you here.
Sharing lunch together	I understand.
Being on time	We missed you.
Sending a thoughtful note	I'm glad you came by.
Bringing a gift	I like that idea!
Sharing an experience	I think you can.
Accepting praise	Welcome.
Giving wait-time	I like what you did.
	Welcome back.

(pp. 132-33)

Invitational education can be applied at a number of levels. Of course, it starts with the inviting teacher who is central to the success of invitational education. However, invitational education goes beyond the teacher, as Purkey and Novak (1984) provide suggestions for how food service professionals, principals, secretaries, counsellors, and school bus drivers can also be inviting. If these people work together they can develop the inviting school, which allows the student to intereact with school personnel in the most satisfying manner. The inviting school has the following characteristics (pp. 96-98):

1. Respect for individual uniqueness. Each student is viewed as unique and capable. Student involvement in the evaluation process is encouraged and "errors are viewed as a source of information rather than as a sign of failure" (p. 96).
2. Co-operative spirit. The inviting school encourages students to participate in the life of the school by tutoring other students and being involved in the decision-making process. Co-operation tends to be emphasized over competition and the use of the learning team approach is very congruent with the inviting school.
3. Sense of belonging. The inviting school values community warmth and togetherness. Both students and teachers feel a commitment to the school and think in terms of *our* school. Teachers care for their students so that students feel part of the classroom and school community.
4. Pleasing Habitat. Teachers and students work together to provide a pleasant interior and exterior to the school. "Extra efforts are made to ensure that lighting, acoustic qualities, temperature, room design, window areas, furniture arrange-

ment, colors, use of space, displays, all make a contribution to an appealing and comfortable setting'' (p. 97).

5. Positive Expectations. Similar to control theory, Purkey and Novak claim that learning is something that happens primarily inside the person. Teachers and school staff view students in a positive manner and students are encouraged to make decisions in what they study and how fast they will learn.

Purkey and Novak claim that the inviting school is much like the inviting family and they call it the inviting family school. The school is similar to the family in that it attempts to provide a warm, caring environment where students can feel comfortable and grow. Listed below are some inviting signs and physical environments:

Inviting Signs	*Inviting Qualities*
Please Use Sidewalks	Fresh paint
Welcome	Pleasant smells
Visitor Parking	Living plants
Please Leave Message	Attractive, up-to-date bulletin boards
Open, Come In	Soft Lighting
No Appointment Necessary	Big and soft pillows
Please Use Other Door	Lots of books
Thank You for Not Smoking	Fresh air
Come Back Soon	Fireplace
Open House	Comfortable furniture
We're Glad You're Here	Rocking Chair
Handicapped Parking	Flowers on the desk
Sorry I Missed You, Please	Open doors
Call Back	Candy jar with candy
Vistors Welcome	Soft music
	Attractive pictures

(pp. 134-35)

Invitational education has been criticized for ignoring problems such as racial discrimination and social inequality. For example, McLaren (1986) states: ''By remaining signally untutored or purposefully silent with respect to the role of schools in the reproduction of the status quo, in the colonization of student subjectivities, and in the proletarianization of teachers, the authors fail to situate their pedagogical concerns within a broader problematic, one that understands how classrooms can be truly humanized only when there exists greater social justice and economic equality in the larger society'' (p. 91). Novak (1986) responds by asking: ''Where and how does a person begin to deal with such problems of magnitude? Does someone have to deal with everything before he or she can deal with anything?'' (p. 98). In other words, faced with a class of thirty-five students how does the teacher begin to deal with the issues raised by McLaren? Novak sees Invitational Education as only a beginning in dealing with the problems that confront the teacher and society.

Social Literacy Training. Alfred Alschuler (1980) has developed an approach to developing school community, based on the work of Paulo Freire (1972), that addresses some of the issues raised by McLaren. Freire's work has been an inspiration to many social-oriented educators who desire major reforms both in school and society. Alschuler used Freire's model to develop a very practical approach to creating a sense of community within schools.

Alschuler claims that there are three major principles in Freire's philosophy. The first involves creating "a world in which it is easier to love" (1972, p. 24). Freire focusses on oppressive social and economic conditions that make it difficult for people to realize their potential as human beings. Oppression involves a situation where one group gets a disproportionate amount of capital or labor for what they contribute to another group or to the economy. For example, it is oppressive when a group of landowners hire workers at very low wages while they reap huge profits. Alschuler also feels school can be oppressive when educators control all the resources (for example, grades and rewards) and do not allow the students to have any control over their own learning. This type of environment makes it difficult for teachers and students to interact in an open, caring way.

The second principle is developing the ability of people to create their own world. Freire argues that people learn to create a world in which it is easier to love in three stages. In the first stage, the *magical-conforming,* people do not recognize the oppression and are passive. At this stage teachers tend to say "kids will always act that way" and because of this belief will make few efforts to encourage positive student growth. In the second stage, the *naive-reforming*, people believe that all difficulties lie with the individual and do not look at system rules and norms. A teacher at this stage will blame himself or herself for problems he or she is having rather than connecting one's behavior to the surrounding context. Although some problems can be solved at the individual level, more serious difficulties may be related to school procedures and norms that exist in the school. In the third stage, the *critical-transforming*, the people realize that they must critique the institutions that govern their lives and collaborate to change those institutions. At this stage teachers work to identify and solve problems. Teachers do not work in isolation, which can happen so often in schools, but work together to improve their instructional and classroom management strategies.

The third principle of Freire's philosophy and social literacy training is developing problem-solving strategies to deal with conflict and oppression. At the heart of problem-solving strategies are three processes. First, the teachers or students name the important conflicts. This can involve generating a list of key words that characterize the conflict or problem. Second, the teachers or students analyse the system causes of conflict. The problem-solvers try to get behind the difficulty to examine the norms and systematic nature of the conflict. In the third step the problem-solvers engage in collaborative action to deal with the difficulty.

Social literacy training involves a variety of strategies to create community within schools. Sometimes these strategies can involve teachers meeting together in small groups to deal with problems. Some of the solutions developed by social literacy groups are:

— One group wanted to reduce referrals to the office. Instead of sending students to the vice-principal, the teachers in one social literacy group made a "mutual aid agreement." Disruptive incidents were defused by sending the student to another teacher's class or having one of the teachers in the Social Literacy group come into another teacher's class to help deal with the problem. Referrals in this school were reduced by 75 percent.

— Three teachers in one Social Literacy group identified the teaching of geography as a problem. They were then able to meet regularly to develop more relevant curriculum in this subject area.

— Some teachers were concerned about new legislation whereby special education students were to be "mainstreamed" into regular classrooms. This Social Literacy group worked with special education teachers to develop an in-service program for the regular classroom teacher. During this process, they focussed on developing new methods for individualizing instruction.

— In one junior high school the students moved from class to class as one group. The Social Literacy group in that school felt that the scheduling tended to limit student options and "fix them into a narrow social role." The teachers approached a university professor to help them install flexible scheduling with the assistance of a computer.

— A Social Literacy group identified the use of the intercom as a problem in the school. Its use was leading to long disruptions in the classroom. The teachers met with the principal, who agreed to limit the use of the intercom.

— Teachers set up a "care" room in the school. Teachers who participated in this project were entitled to send students to the room, where there was a teacher for special help. The room also provided a cooling-down period for students.

— Women in one school formed a consciousness-raising group to deal with the problem of sexism in the school.

Alschuler comments on these examples:

> These examples illustrate several unique characteristics of socially literate methods of reducing the discipline problem: (1) Socially Literate solutions do not blame individuals. Individuals cooperate to change the rules and roles of the system. (2) Social Literacy leads to multileveled solutions that win peace in interpersonal, classroom, and schoolwide war games. (3) Socially Literate solutions yield a broad range of outcomes related to better discipline — fewer classroom conflicts, more learning of the subject matter discipline, greater disciple-ship and increased personal discipline. (p. 42)

In order to facilitate problem-solving, Freire (1972) encourages the use of dialogue, which is facilitated by six conditions (also cited in Alschuler 1980):

1. Love — "Dialogue cannot exist . . . in the absence of a profound love for the world and for human beings" (Freire 1972, p. 78).

2. Humility — "Dialogue cannot exist without humility . . . Dialogue, as the encounter of human beings addressed to the common task of learning and acting, is broken if the parties (or one of them) lack humility. How can I dialogue if I always project ignorance onto others and never perceive my own? At the point of encounter . . . there are only people who are attempting, together, to learn more than they now know" (ibid., pp. 78-79).

3. Faith — "Dialogue . . . requires an intense faith in people, faith in the power to make and re-make, to create and re-create, faith in their vocation to be more fully human" (ibid., p. 79).

4. Trust — ''Founding itself on love, humility and faith, dialogue becomes a horizontal relationship of which mutual trust between the dialoguers is the logical consequence'' (ibid., pp. 79-80).

5. Hope — ''As the encounter of people seeking to be more fully human, dialogue cannot be carried on in a climate of hopelessness. If the dialoguers expect nothing to come of their effort, their encounter will be empty and sterile, bureaucratic and tedious'' (ibid., p. 80).

6. Critical thinking — ''Finally, true dialogue cannot exist unless the dialoguers engage in critical thinking . . . For the naive thinker, the important thing is accommodation to this normalized 'today.' For the critic, the important thing is the continuing transformation of reality on behalf of the continuing humanization of people'' (ibid., pp. 80-81).

These conditions are necessary for dialogue and are also fundamental to creating a caring school community. Dialogue also involves speaking what Freire calls ''true words.'' True words are similar to Ashton-Warner's key vocabulary in that they are rooted in the lives of the students and are often related to problems they are confronting. It is very important that teachers not engage in pseudo-dialogue such as asking questions where they already know the answers or questions that seem to promote intellectual oneupmanship rather than collaborative problem-solving.

Alschuler (1980) gives examples of different teachers who allow students to participate in decision-making. One teacher who taught a reading class at the junior high level had one class that was extremely bored so he discussed with the students ways in which the class could be improved. As a result of the discussion, part of the class time was devoted to free reading, where students could choose the books they wanted to read, while the remaining time was devoted to working on specific reading skills. After devoting time to free reading, the teacher found that the ''students have worked harder and more conscientiously on the work and have accomplished more in the way of mastery than when almost 100 percent of the time was supposedly allotted to learning skills, almost none to free reading. . . . Grades are up and so are attitudes and relationships'' (p. 153).

Student–Community Connections

Community Involvement/Social Action Projects. Many programs have been developed which encourage contact between the student and the surrounding community. Generally, there are three types of programs that facilitate contact between school and community. The most common type is the apprenticeship program where students work in the business community. The prime focus is on developing job skills and on preparing the student for future employment in industry. Sometimes this type of project can be transmission-oriented if there is little opportunity for students to reflect on or have input into what is happening.

A second type of project is community involvement or service-oriented contact. Here the student has some form of contact with a community service agency. For example, students can work in day care agencies or observe court proceedings. In Ontario, students have been able to obtain high school credits in the Community Involvement Program (CIP). This program has three components and one component involves direct contact with a community agency. A second component consists of in-class discussion on issues related to the community work. For example, the students can discuss public policy issues (for example, the value and feasibility of universal day care). The third aspect of the CIP consists of an independent research project that is related to the community contact and class discussions.

Community involvement is also part of social action programs (Newmann, 1975), but these programs advance the student another step by encouraging the student to effect some change in the life of the community. In social action the student develops a set of goals and then works for support of those goals through organizing, petitioning, and writing letters. Newmann's program attempts to develop civic competencies as he is convinced that our schools tend to reinforce citizen apathy in society. A specific program for developing civic competency is outlined by Newmann, Bertocci, and Landsness (1977). The program is designed for grade 11 or 12 students to achieve the following goals:

1. Communicate effectively in spoken and written language.
2. Collect and logically interpret information on problems of public concern.
3. Describe political-legal decision-making processes.
4. Rationally justify personal decisions on controversial public issues and strategies for action with reference to principles of justice and constitutional democracy.
5. Work cooperatively with others.
6. Discuss concrete personal experiences of self and others in ways that contribute to resolution of personal dilemmas encountered in civic action and that relate these experiences to more general human issues.
7. Use selected technical skills as they are required for exercise of influence on specific issues. (p. 6)

The program consists of six courses. The courses are briefly described below:

1. *Political–legal process course,* three mornings a week, for fourteen weeks during the first semester. Here the student would learn the "realities" of the political system. There would be an examination of the formal structure of the system as well as of informal processes like lobbying and bargaining. Students would also have firsthand opportunities to observe these processes in action through field experiences. These experiences could include attending meetings and conducting interviews. The course could also focus on developing skills in data gathering and drawing valid conclusions. Moral deliberation skills would also be dealt with in this part of the program, and the student would have the opportunity to develop position papers on controversial issues.

2. *Communications course,* four afternoons a week, for sixteen weeks during the first semester. Here the student would develop skills in written, spoken, and nonverbal communications. Skills would be applied to four contexts: intrapersonal, interpersonal, group, and the public. For example, the student could work on interpersonal helping skills, such as empathy and regard, as well as group skills, such as problem identification and clarification. Emphasis would also be given to building trust and group cohesion so that the student could work with others.

3. *Community service internship,* two mornings a week, for fourteen weeks during the first semester. Students would perform volunteer work in social agencies, government bodies, and public interest groups.

> The intern might work in an understudy relationship to one adult for the entire period (e.g., as an aide to a TV news reporter), might have short tours of duty among different groups (e.g., helping in several different departments in an environmental protection agency), might be involved in special projects (e.g., gathering data for a neighborhood organization), might offer direct social services to "clients" (e.g., tutoring young children or assisting the elderly). The placement should expose the student to the daily functioning of the agency, should provide opportunities for the student to communicate actively with agency people (rather than passively observe them), and should require that the student make a contribution to the agency's mission. (pp. 48-49)

As the students become involved in internship, they could analyse institutional processes of the agency in the political-legal process course and work on relevant language skills in the communications course. One afternoon per week students could "share their volunteer experiences, discuss common problems, and begin to explore issues that might develop into the citizen action project for the second semester" (p. 10).

4. *Citizen action project,* four mornings a week, for ten weeks during the second semester. In this part of the program the students would work to affect public policy.

Projects could include working for political candidates, establishing special youth institutions, revising administrative regulations, lobbying for legislation, and so forth. The issue could concern national, state, or local agencies, including the schools; for example, student rights within a school, zoning provisions to protect the environment, consumer protection, interracial co-operation, improved social services for youth in trouble.

The project could develop from the first semester's work. During the project the students could also take "skill clinics" on such matters as canvassing techniques, negotiation skills, fund-raising, and how to run a meeting. "Project counseling sessions" would also be offered to deal with various issues that arise during the project and would provide psychological support to the students.

5. *Action in literature project,* two afternoons a week, for ten weeks during the second semester. This course has a more general focus than the others and deals with such issues as: What is meaningful social change? Can an individual make a difference? How should humans govern themselves? These questions can be pursued through fiction, biography, poetry, and drama. For example, students might read a biography of Gandhi, Thoreau on civil disobedience, a novel such as *All the King's Men,* and the writings of James Baldwin.

6. *Public message.* Each citizen action group would develop a final "message" on their activities to be shared with their peers and the public at large. Students would study the various media and prepare a report on their activities for one of them. The emphasis would be on what had been accomplished in the project, and the intention would be to interpret the students' experience to the public.

Student projects. Three types of community involvement projects are identified for the program. (1) In exploratory research students investigate the community, gathering information through field trips, interviews, guest speakers, informal observation in community institutions, and other means (Newmann, 1975, p. 143). (2) Volunteer service places the student in a direct helping relationship to others. For example, students work in homes for the elderly, day-care centres, tutoring programs, and neighborhood cleanup campaigns. (3) Social action projects ask the student to take an advocate position and attempt to effect change congruent with that position. Newmann suggests that a developmental relationship might exist with the three projects. Exploratory research is more self-oriented as the individual goes into the community to gather relevant information. Volunteer service requires more participation as the individual may help or care for others. Finally, in the advocacy role, students emerge as autonomous agents who engage in concerns that relate to a broader social context.

References

Alschuler, A. *School Disciplines: A Socially Literate Solution.* New York: McGraw Hill, 1980.

Freire, P. *Pedagogy of the Oppressed.* New York: Harper and Row, 1956.

Glasser, W. *Control Theory in the Classroom.* New York: Harper and Row, 1986.

Glasser, W. *Schools without Failure.* New York: Harper and Row, 1969.

Gough, P. B. "The Key to Improving Schools: An Interview with William Glasser." *Phi Delta Kappan* 68 (1987), 656-62.

Johnson, D.; Johnson, R.; and Holubec, E. J. *Circles of Learning.* Revised edition. Edina, Minnesota: Interaction Book Co., 1986.

McLaren, P. "Interrogating Invitational Education." *Interchange* 17 (1986), 90-95.

Newmann, F. W. *Education for Citizen Action: Challenge for Secondary Curriculum.* Berkeley, Calif.: McCutchan, 1975.

Newmann, F. W.; Bertocci, T.; and Landsness, R. M. *Skills in Citizen Action: An English-Social Studies Program for Secondary Schools.* Skokie, Ill.: National Textbook, 1977.

Novak, J. "From Interrogation to Conversation." *Interchange* 17 (1986), 96-99.

Purkey, W., and Novak. J. *Inviting School Success: A Self-Concept Approach to Teaching and Learning.* Belmont, Calif.: Wadsworth Publishing, 1984.

Smith, R. A. "A Teacher's View of Cooperative Learning." *Phi Delta Kappan* 68 (1987), 663-66.

9

Self-Connections

In defining the holistic curriculum I have stressed connections and relationships as the main vehicle for realizing the student's true nature. This is in keeping with Steiner's (1976) suggestion that "moving from one thing to another in a way that connects one thing with another is more beneficial than anything else for the development of spirit and soul and even body" (p. 173). It is also possible to connect students with the Self directly. In this chapter, I would like to suggest a few directions for this process which include Steiner's theory of child development, meditation, and studying world religions at the secondary level.

Steiner's Theory of Child Development

It is time that educators outside of the Waldorf movement begin to look closely at the work of Rudolf Steiner. There are two basic reasons for examining Steiner's work. First, Steiner's model is holistic in that it includes intellectual, physical, emotional, and spiritual growth. The developmental model which has been most heavily promoted by educators has been Jean Piaget's, but this model is primarily cognitive. Although Piaget also did research on the child's moral development, his work is basically concerned with how the child's cognitive processes develop. Steiner's model, however, is not limited to cognition, but links changes in the child's thought to physical and emotional development. Most importantly, Steiner shows how the Self emerges through different periods of the child's development.

Another important reason for focussing on Steiner's theory is he is the only developmentalist who is also an educator. Piaget was a psychologist, and it was left to the educators to develop the implications of his theory; Steiner, on the other hand, actually developed a curriculum from kindergarten through high school based on his theories.

Applying Steiner's work to public education presents certain problems and opportunities. One difficulty is that his work has received little attention and there will simply have to be a great deal of work to make his ideas well known. These ideas also will have to be articulated in an open manner free from any hint of dogmatism; in other words, his theory should be viewed as a hypothesis to be tested by experience, rather than as dogma that must be followed by ritual. Mary Caroline Richards, in an interview with the author (Miller, 1987), said that when she reads Steiner it tends to facilitate her creativity while some of her Steiner colleagues tend to close off. Those of us outside the Waldorf movement have the opportunity to look at Steiner's theory critically and also to link his work with other holistic approaches to education. I think that sometimes Waldorf teachers may be reluctant to try something different if it is not recommended by Steiner, but I think teachers should feel free to experiment as long as it is within a holistic context. Much of the material described in the second part of this book, including metaphor, visualization, holistic thinking, and mindfulness, could be related to Steiner's model of development. For example, visualization would be very appropriate during the etheric stage, since this period of development is so concerned with imagination. Sylvia Ashton-Warner's organic approach to reading and co-operative learning would also seem to be congruent with this stage. Various approaches to holistic thinking might be most appropriate during adolescence, since this is the time that intellectual development becomes predominant in Steiner's model. Social action and community service activities of the Foxfire type might also be related to this stage of development.

Of course, there is a danger that Steiner's work could be watered down by such an approach, but I believe that the risk is worth taking. I feel that Steiner would want teachers to teach from their centres rather than from a plan, even if it is Steiner's plan. Of course, there is much to be gained from also following the Steiner curriculum, which provides a solid base on which to build. One building block for the Waldorf curriculum is the fairy tale, and Diana Hughes (1987) has discussed the role of fairy tales in relation to moral education. As indicated earlier, the etheric stage of development is characterized by imagination and the need for moral absolutes and these qualities are also found in fairy tales. Hughes (1987) says:

> How then does the fairy tale reflect a child's real psychological and emotional being? Rudolf Steiner demonstrated that the fundamental mood of early childhood (to age 7) proceeds from the unconscious assumption that the whole world is of a moral nature. While avoiding all those arguments as to whether the child is born moral or immoral, one has only to linger near the express line-up at the supermarket or customs clearance at the airport to appreciate the child's innate sense of the good, the just and the true. (''Mommy, you've got thirteen things, not eight!'' ''What about the watch you bought for Uncle John?'') (p. 11)

Fairy tales speak directly to this innate morality of the child; there is a moral order in the fairy tale where evil is inevitably punished. Hughes claims that the fact that ''evil is always self-consuming is usually a source of reassurance and comfort, if not downright delight, to the healthy child'' (p. 12). At the same time the child can also identify with the hero's struggles and how he or she is able to realize a deeper happiness through the struggle with malevolent forces. Carlgren (1976) claims:

> However, what matters most is that children should experience how the benefi- cent powers in the world rule supreme, and how they enable the characters of the fairy tales, be they kings or hunters, princes or soldiers, to develop virtues such as courage, perseverance, loyalty or a sense of justice. For in this way the ''Happy End'' imbues the children with reassurance and confidence that the evil in the world can be and must be overcome and that renewed strength and a deeper happiness are the just reward for an honest struggle. (p. 85)

The fairy tales stimulate the inner life of the child since it is rich in images which stir the child's own imagination. Fairy tales allow the child to put himself or herself in the shoes of the person struggling with evil and to see the struggle unfold within the mind's eye as the story is told. And it is important that the story be told. Fairy tales developed in an oral tradition have the greatest effect when related in that context. By stimulating empathy and imagination, fairy tales build the foundation for compassionate imagination which is so linked with the Self. Since the Self is rooted in the connectedness among all beings, enlivening empathy and imagination in the young child provides a basis for wisdom and compassion in the adult.

World Religions

During adolescence the conscious search for meaning takes hold. I believe that by studying the world religions this search can be stimulated and perhaps some answers provided. Some of the traditional themes of such a course have been identified by Myrna Dales (1987) and include:

Some Topics To Be Explored

in the "Themes in World Religions" Course

- *Introduction*—How does one define "religion"? Does the concept of religion necessarily imply belief in a god or gods? (For example, can Humanism be considered a religion?) Does there seem to be a trend against or toward faith of some kind? Is religion an "illusion" (Sigmund Freud) or "the highest reality" (P. Yogananda)? Which beliefs have developed into "world" religions, and why have they spread?

- *An Examination of Creation Stories*—Examples can be discussed from Ancient Israel, Mesopotamia, Persia, Egypt, Greece, India, Tibet, and China, etc. Which of these creation stories have been retained in religions existing today (e.g., "Genesis" in the Hebrew *Old Testament*)?

- *The Significance of Holy Days, Rituals, and Celebrations in Major Religions*— The character, ceremonies, and importance of the Hebrew, Muslim, and Hindu New Year, Christmas and Easter in Christianity, and the birth and enlightenment of the Buddha will be examined.

- *Religious Symbols*—Are these basically universal (C. G. Jung), or are they unique in each religion? With what connotations do such symbols as the tree, the mountain, the serpent, light, and water appear in Judaism, Christianity, Islam, Hinduism, Buddhism, etc.?

- *Religious Leaders, Prophets, and Holy Men*—The following will be among those whose importance to their religions will be discussed: Abraham, Moses, Isaiah, John the Baptist, Jesus, Mohammed, the Brahmins, Buddha, Lao-tze, and Confucius.

- *Concepts of the Godhead*—In which religions have religious teachers been deified?
  In which faiths is the Godhead regarded as immanent or transcendent, or both?
  If God is transcendent, is He seen as a loving father or a stern judge?

- *Scriptures*—Which religions regard their scriptures as divine revelations and which as teachings?
  The *Old* and *New Testaments*, the *Koran*, the *Upanishads* (Hinduism) and the *Tripitaka* (Buddhism) will be discussed.

- *Conduct and Morality*—How does each religion view man's obligations to the Godhead or religious leaders? What rules of conduct must be followed in dealing with one's fellow man, according to The Ten Commandments, Jesus's teachings, the Buddha's Eightfold Path, and the Hindu Code of Manu?

- *Various Religious Viewpoints of Man's True Purpose in Life*—Which religion(s) stress the living of a good life on earth, the preparation for a world to come, or an escape from the cycle of rebirths?

- *Man's Position with Respect to Other Forms of Life*—Does man hold dominion over all other earthly creatures (Judeo-Christian tradition)? Is man one with all creation (Taoism, Hinduism, Buddhism)?

- *Death and Concepts of an After-life*—Concepts of heaven, hell, nirvana, resurrection, and reincarnation as they apply to the religions being studied.

- *Art and Architecture Inspired by World Religions*—Religious paintings and sculptures will be viewed and related to the concepts which engendered them. The significance will be discussed of such structures as Solomon's Temple, various cathedrals, Islamic mosques and Hindu places of worship.

- *The Encounters of Religions*—Topics will include Islamic and Christian encounters with Hinduism, and the changes in Buddhism as it moved into China and Japan.

- *Conclusion: Emerging Trends in the Field of Religion*—Topics include: "Back to Christ" movements, the revival of old nature religions, Western adaptations of Eastern religions such as the Hare Krishna sect, and explorations of the possibility of a universal religion. ■

(*Ethics in Education*, Vol. 6, No. 3 (January 1987), p. 8.)

These themes can be explored by reading the sacred texts and visiting religious festivals and services of the various faiths. Dales, who teaches world religions in Toronto, comments:

> In the fall, we usually attend the celebration for the Hindu mother goddess, conveniently located at Harbourfront. In the spring, the birth of the Buddha service offers a wonderful glimpse into Shin Buddhism. Zen meditation groups have provided speakers who have answered questions before and after services. Mosque visits have given a sense of Muslim worship far more vivid than that obtainable from books. Synagogues and churches have welcomed student groups. (p. 7)

I would supplement Dales's approach with a study of the mystical thread of each faith and how the notion of the Self (see chapter 2) is articulated within each tradition. The student can see the commonality of the major faiths, particularly with reference to the idea of connectedness and selflessness. Related to this notion is the idea of spiritual practice, which is essential to realizing the Self. Students can examine and even experiment with various forms of spiritual practice which are fundamental to realizing our true nature. Spiritual practice brings faith into one's daily life in the most immediate and direct way as the seeker meditates, visualizes, or prays not just on Sunday but every day, or ideally every moment, as a vehicle for awakening. The notion of spiritual practice, then, makes religion concrete and specific.

Meditation

Meditation in its various forms is probably the most time-honored way to realize who we are. Jack Kornfield, in an interview (Miller; 1987), explains the purpose of meditation in a context appropriate to this book when he says:

> Most of us are disconnected; we are disconnected from our hearts and our bodies, from the mind and its ways, from one another, from the earth and from the universal laws and truths. Through meditation we can reconnect with all of these factors. Through meditation we can rediscover love, oneness and freedom. Many people meditate for other reasons — for example, to deal with pain and to understand suffering. However, if one practices with an open heart and mind, meditation eventually leads to a oneness, a deep connectedness.

Meditation involves a quieting and focussing of the mind. When we quiet and focus the mind we move to a more receptive mode of consciousness — the listening, intuitive mind. The listening mind is characterized by a still, concentrated awareness. In contrast, in the active mode of consciousness the mind is continually chattering, planning, and manipulating. It is possible to see the active mind as a reflection of our egos, which are usually attempting to manipulate the universe according to our own need for gratification. The listening mind is a reflection of our Self or Centre which occasionally has glimpses of the unity of things and our connectedness to this unity.

It is possible to approach meditation from a number of levels. At one level many people use meditation as a vehicle to deal with stress. There is plenty of evidence that meditation practice, can lead to lower blood pressure, a slower rate of breathing, and a general slowing of metabolic processes (Benson, 1976). The most likely reason for this slowdown is that during meditation practice the individual focusses on one aspect of awareness while during the day consciousness is shifting from one stimulus to another countless times. For example, at home where I am supposed to be relaxing after a long day, I can be reading the newspaper, watching the TV, and talking to my wife at the same time. In meditation we settle down for a while as we simply focus on our breathing. Below are two breath meditations which could be used with most students.

> Sit comfortably in an upright position. You can sit in a chair or on a cushion; however, you should keep your back fairly erect. Close your eyes. Now begin to notice the flow of the breath coming in and out of the nose. This meditation involves counting the breaths to yourself as you exhale. You inhale, and then count one as you exhale. Inhale, and count two. You do this up to ten and begin over. Don't worry if you lose track of the counting. Simply, return to one and start over.

> Sit comfortably in a upright position and close your eyes. Now focus on the flow of the breath out of the nostrils. As you inhale, mentally note ''in'' and as you exhale mentally note ''out.'' If the sensations rise such as an itch, note the sensation and return to the breath. You will have thoughts, so again be mindful of the thought and then return to the breath. Do not try to shut out thoughts, merely be aware of them as they arise in your mind.

Each of the above meditations can be done for ten to twenty minutes each day. Using meditation as a vehicle to counter stress is working at Vaughn's physical level of intuition. However, the meditations described above can open the student to all levels.

At the emotional level we can use meditation to help the process of personal integration and the development of self-concept as we need to link a healthy ego to the Self. Here we can repeat a phrase over and over to create a beneficial emotional state. The phrase is sometimes called a mantra. An example of a phrase designed to enhance one's self-image is found in the book *100 Ways to Enhance Self-Concept in the Classroom.*

> No matter what you say or do to me, I'm still a worthwhile person!
>
> Ask the students to close their eyes and repeat in unison with you the chant: "No matter what you say or do to me, I'm still a worthwhile person!" This seemingly simple exercise has a very powerful impact if done repeatedly, it implants a new seed thought in each of the students; it acts as an antidote to all the negative thoughts and statements already implanted in their thinking.
>
> A way to heighten the effect of this exercise is to ask students to imagine the face of someone who has put them down in some way in the past — a parent, teacher, coach, friend, fellow student, Girl Scout leader, policeman, etc. — each time they begin to say "No matter. . ." Have them stick out their chins and repeat the sentence strongly and convincingly.
>
> After they get the hang of it you might interject statements like "You're stupid, ugly, etc." and let them respond to these with "No matter what you say or do to me, I'm still a worthwhile person." (Canfield and Wells, 1976, p. 69)

Meditations that are more intellectually oriented are appropriate for the older adolescent and focus on contemplation. One classic meditation is to reflect on the question "Who am I?" Other meditations can involve inquiry into the nature of emotions such as fear and anger. In these meditations the student sits quietly for a few minutes focussing on the question in an attentive yet open manner so that responses can arise intuitively.

In using meditation with students keep things simple. Meditation is most easily integrated into health and physical education as relaxation exercises. Through relaxation, however, the student can access his or her centre. At the spiritual level it is possible to explore some simple non-sectarian exercises that focus on realizing the connectedness among all beings. For example, have students repeat the following phrases to themselves.

— May I be well, happy, and peaceful.
— May all beings in this room be well, happy, and peaceful.
— May all beings in this school be well, happy, and peaceful.
— May all beings in this neighborhood be well, happy, and peaceful.
— May all beings in this state or province be well, happy, and peaceful.
— May all beings in this country be well, happy, and peaceful.
— May all beings in this hemisphere be well, happy, and peaceful.
— May all beings on this planet be well, happy, and peaceful.
— May all beings in this universe be well, happy, and peaceful.

Doing this exercise over time can facilitate a deep sense of connectedness with others and identification with all beings on this globe.

In *The Compassionate Teacher* and in the next chapter I discuss the importance of meditation to the teacher. Holistic education should come from the deepest place in the teacher, and meditation and other forms of spiritual practice are fundamental to this process. If the teacher is not engaged in some effort to connect with the Self, then any attempt at holistic education will indeed be hollow.

References

Benson, H. *The Relaxation Response.* New York: Avon Books, 1976.

Calgren, F. *Education towards Freedom.* East Grinstead: Lanthorn Press, 1976.

Canfield, Jack, and Wells, Harold. *100 Ways to Enhance Self-Concept in the Classroom.* Englewood Cliffs, N.J.: Prentice-Hall, 1976.

Dales, Myrna. "The Teaching of World Religions." *Ethics in Education* 6 (January 1987), 6-9.

Hughes, Diana. "Fairy Tales: A Basis for Moral Education." *Ethics in Education* 6 (March 1987), 10-13.

Miller, J. *The Compassionate Teacher.* Englewood Cliffs, N.J.: Prentice-Hall, 1981.

Miller, J. "New Age Pilgrims." Unpublished manuscript, 1987.

Steiner, Rudolf. *Practical Advice for Teachers.* London: Rudolf Steiner Press, 1976.

10

The Holistic Teacher

The holistic curriculum has its roots in the consciousness of authentic and caring teachers. Of course, it is possible to develop a long list of qualities that teachers should have, but these laundry lists are usually not very helpful. In this last chapter I would like to explore what it means to be an authentic and caring teacher and briefly look at how holistic education can be brought into schools.

Authenticity

There are several forms of authenticity — psychological, moral, and holistic. Before exploring these forms it is important to look at existentialism, because philosophers such as Kierkegaard and Heidegger did much to bring the concept of authenticity to our attention.

Existentialism/Kierkegaard. Sören Kierkegaard has been identified as a precursor of modern existentialism. He was deeply concerned with what constitutes authentic existence. Kierkegaard discusses three levels of existence; each level could be seen as being more authentic than the previous stage.

Kierkegaard's first level is the *aesthetic.* The aesthete lives only for the pleasurable moment. The aesthete avoids facing the fundamental realities of existence and instead runs from himself or herself in the search for pleasure. Kierkegaard also refers to the intellectual aesthete who tries to stand outside life and beholds it as a spectacle. The intellectual "aesthete" watches, contemplates, and speculates but does not engage life.

The second level is the *ethical*, and Kierkegaard argues that at this level real moral growth can occur. In *Either/Or,* Kierkegaard states:

> I should like to say that in making a choice it is not so much a question of choosing the right as of the energy, the consciousness, the pathos with which one chooses. Thereby the personality announces its inner infinity, and thereby, in turn, the personality is consolidated. Therefore, even if a man were to choose the wrong, he will nevertheless discover, precisely by reason of the energy with which he chose, that he has chosen the wrong. For, the choice being made with the whole inwardness of his personality, his nature is purified and he himself

brought into immediate relation to the eternal Power whose omnipresence interpenetrates the whole of existence . . . (Kierkegaard, 1967, in Greene, pp. 99-100)

The ethical person, then, does not get lost in the immediate moment but moves to a greater level of authentic involvement. Right and wrong are not viewed in an abstract way but as directly related to one's inner being.

Kierkegaard's third level is the *religious*. At the ethical level it is possible to conceive of ethical rules which are universal. The religious person, however, may be called upon to break the universal rule. Kierkegaard refers to the example of Abraham's near sacrifice of his son Isaac. If a person is called upon to break a universal rule, the individual does so with what Kierkegaard calls "fear and trembling" and not with the arrogance of Nietzsche's superman. At the centre of Kierkegaard's philosophy lies the belief that the individual is higher than the universal. Barrett (1962) comments:

> The universal rule of ethics, precisely because it is universal, cannot comprehend totally me, the individual, in my concreteness. Where then as an abstract rule it commands something that goes against my deepest self (but it has to be my deepest self, and herein the fear and trembling of the choice reside), then I feel compelled out of conscience — a religious conscience superior to the ethical — to transcend that rule. I am compelled to make an exception because I myself am an exception; that is, a concrete being whose existence can never be completely subsumed under any universal or even system of universals. (p. 167)

Kierkegaard's conception of authenticity and morality are linked with the individual person in a very specific and concrete manner. Indeed, it is only the individual and the concrete choices that he or she faces that allows for the expression of authenticity.

Heidegger is another individual who discussed the concept of authenticity. Heidegger develops the concept of the authentic and inauthentic life in his work *Being and Time*. An authentic approach to life means that the individual makes choices with a full awareness of the fundamental conditions of human life. For Heidegger (1972), these conditions include being responsible for what one is and does, and facing one's own death. Death, then, is a central consideration in relation to Heidegger's concept of authenticity.

> Death is a possibility of Being that each Dasein (person) must itself take over. With death Dasein stands before itself in its most proper potentiality for Being. What is involved in this possibility is nothing less than the being no longer able to be "there." When Dasein stands before itself as this possibility it is fully directed toward its very own potentiality for Being. Standing before itself in this way all relations in it to other Daseins are dissolved. This most proper, nonrelational possibility is at the same time the most extreme. As potentiality for Being, Dasein cannot surmount the possibility of death. Death is the possibility of the unqualified impossibility of Dasein. Death thus reveals itself as the most proper, nonrelational, insurmountable possibility. (p. 250)

Like Kierkegaard, Heidegger believes that authentic existence is a self-chosen existence which is shaped by the individual making his or her own decisions. An authentic existence involves looking directly at one's life and not evading our fundamental responsibilities. The existentialists are helpful in focussing on our subjectivity and in helping us to live authentically in relation to this subjectivity. In Satre's view it is "bad faith" to reject our subjectivity and adopt roles based on social expectations. The existentialists remind teachers that they cannot hide behind the role of teacher; instead, they are primarily human beings who are vulnerable and open in their subjectivity. It is so easy to close ourselves off and confront the student in our roles rather than from a place of subjective openness. An English teacher, Steven Urkowitz, put this very well:

> I think a lot of teachers are too scared. When they're in front of a class they're defending their authority. They don't want to show their vulnerability to artistic or intellectual challenges. They don't want to say, "I get excited about this," any more than they would like to sit down in front of the class and say, "I really groove on hot dogs." Instead they don't let people know. Rather than being responsive members of the culture, they stand up there as the abstracted agents of it. (Macrorie, 1984, p. 105).

Psychological Congruence/Carl Rogers. Rogers was influenced by the existentialists and devoted a great deal of his work to the concept of congruence, genuineness, or realness. He uses these terms interchangeably as they are also interchangeable with authenticity. Rogers (1961) defines congruence in the following manner: "Congruence is the term we have used to indicate an accurate matching of experiencing and awareness. It may be still further extended to cover a matching of experience, awareness, and communication" (p. 339). He (1961) gives the following example of congruence:

> To pick an easily recognizable example take the man who becomes angrily involved in a group discussion. His face flushes, his tone communicates anger, he shakes his finger at his opponent. Yet when a friend says, "Well, let's not get angry about this," he replies, with evident sincerity and surprise, "I'm not angry! I don't have any feeling about this at all! I was just pointing out the logical facts." The other men in the group break out in laughter at this statement.

> What is happening here? It seems clear that at a physiological level he is experiencing anger. This is not matched by his awareness. Consciously he is not experiencing anger, nor is he communicating this (so far as he is consciously aware). There is a real incongruence between experience and awareness, and between experience and communication. (pp. 339-40)

Rogers (1961) develops a hypothesis based on his concept of congruence:

> The greater the congruence of experience, awareness and communication on the part of one individual, the more the ensuing relationship will involve: a tendency toward reciprocal communication with a quality of increasing congruence; a tendency toward more mutually accurate understanding of the communications; improved psychological adjustment and functioning in both parties; mutual satisfaction in the relationship. (p. 344)

Rogers also argues that teachers should be congruent if student growth is to occur. He (1969) states that the most "essential attitude in the facilitation of learning is realness or genuineness." Thus, teachers should be real or genuine in their communications with students. He gives an example of one grade 6 teacher being real with her students:

I find it maddening to live with the mess — with a capital M! No one seems to care except me. Finally, one day I told the children . . . that I am a neat, orderly person by nature and that the mess was driving me to distraction. Did they have a solution? It was suggested there were some volunteers who could clean up . . . I said it didn't seem fair to me to have the same people clean up all the time for others — but it would solve it for me. "Well, some people like to clean," they replied. So that's the way it is. (p. 108)

Rogers does not deal extensively with the problems of congruence for teachers. What if the teacher feels negatively about the subject matter or even about some of the students in his or her class? Does this mean the person should express his or her feelings openly about these matters? Should one always be confronting others with their inner feelings?

Despite these difficulties, Rogers has elaborated on what I call psychological congruence. It is important for teachers to be in touch with themselves, as we have already seen in the Body–Mind chapter. The person who cannot listen to his or her inner life, the psychosomatic, cannot communicate with others.

Moral Congruence. Another form of authenticity is living according to one's espoused values. Once I ran a workshop for the staff of a secondary school who were upset about the students' vulgar language, lack of respect for teachers, and sloppy handwriting. It was no surprise that during the workshop the following behaviors emerged from the teachers — sloppy writing, vulgar language, and not listening to each other. It is important that teachers be prepared to ask the same questions of themselves that they ask of students. Students, particularly adolescents, are quick to pick up on the credibility gap between what teachers say and what they do. If this gap becomes too large the hypocrisy leads to alienation in the school. Teachers should not be rigid role models, but instead engage in self-examination with regard to their own values and behavior.

Holistic Congruence. Holistic congruence refers to being in touch with one's centre. The holistic teacher teaches from the Self. Emerson (1965) expressed this very well:

According to the depth from which you draw your life, such is the depth not only of your strenuous effort, but of your manners and presence. The beautiful nature of the world has here blended your happiness with your power . . . Consent yourself to be an organ of your highest thought, and lo! suddenly you put all men in your debt, and are the fountain of an energy that goes pulsing on with waves of benefit to the borders of society, to the circumference of things. (p. 437)

Emerson is arguing that by developing our inner life as teachers we can be more in touch or congruent with what he called "moral sentiment," which is another term for his "big fellow." In 1869 he wrote, "The first simple foundation of my belief is that the Author of nature has not left himself without a witness in any sane mind: that the moral sentiment speaks to every man the law after which the Universe was made."

A teacher who is holistically authentic realizes there is a link between one's consciousness or inner life and other beings. This connection has been summarized in a Buddhist quotation:

The thought manifests as the word,
The word manifests as the deed,
The deed develops into habit,
And the habit hardens into character.
So watch the thought
And its ways with care,
And let it spring from love
Born out of respect for all beings.

To be fully authentic there must then be a fundamental awakening to our inner life: our thoughts and images and their connection to other beings. By being aware of how thoughts arise in our consciousness we can sense our connectedness to others and to what Emerson called the Oversoul. Various meditative disciplines, of course, focus on developing this awareness. The existentialists whom I cited at the beginning of this chapter also call on us to be aware of our subjectivity. Kierkegaard, for example, argues that this awareness is fundamental to his highest stage of growth, the religious, while Heidegger claims that an awareness of Being leads to a caring for others.

I would argue that psychological congruence, moral congruence, and holistic congruence are important to holistic education. In the past decade many educators have stressed techniques and strategies which have tended to diminish the teacher's Being. Technique is not enough. Even technique supplemented by good theory is not enough. In the final analysis, holistic education should involve both good theory and competent technique but it can only come to life in the authentic presence of the teacher.

Caring

To be holistically authentic is to care, for if we see the connectedness to others then inevitably we care for them as well. Noddings (1984), who has written about caring, claims that our schools are in a "crisis of caring" as "students and teachers are brutally attacked verbally and physically" (p. 181). Again, this crisis reflects the atomization of society and of schools.

How can the teacher care in this crisis? It is not the responsibility of the teacher to engage each student in a deep interpersonal relationship; of course, this is impossible and not even desirable. According to Noddings, "What I must do is to be totally and nonselectively present to the student — to each student — as he addresses me. The time interval may be brief but the encounter is total" (p. 180). In short, teachers should simply learn to *be* with students. In being with students, I am fully present. I am not thinking about what I will be doing after school or even in the next class but I engage each student directly. Students can sense when we are not with them, and if this sense becomes permanent a deep alienation can develop between student and teacher.

Teachers can also show caring by relating subject matter to the interests of the student. If the teacher can make connections between subject matter and student interests the student will often respond by engaging the subject matter more directly. As Noddings notes, the student "may respond by free, vigorous, and happy immersion in his own projects" (p. 181). Suggestions about how the teacher can be inviting (Purkey and Novak, 1984) can also be helpful in showing how teachers care. But caring is not a technique; like authenticity it is rooted in our being.

Marcia Umland talks about how she cares for her kids in an elementary school classroom:

> Teaching in elementary school can be isolating. A teacher can always do badly — just assign things and get the kids to say them back and then make a good presentation when the principal visits the room. When I wanted to spend all that time with those little people in class, I found that the intimacy I had shared with my peers in college in the sixties was carried over into my classroom. I cared about the students and couldn't stand to sit in the teachers' lounge where they were gossiping about their students . . .
>
> I get exhausted, but not burned out. Sometimes I'm dropping my dream for a day or two, but most days I'm on, and stunned by the kids. Lately I've realized that in setting up a classroom at last I've given myself permission to form a society I'd like to live in. (Macrorie, 1959, pp. 155-61)

As Umland relates, caring can result in the classroom becoming a community. By caring for students, they eventually feel comfortable in relating to one another and to the teacher.

The Holistic Principal

How do we bring about the holistic curriculum in schools? In recent years there has been literature on implementation and how we can attempt to bring about the programs we want in schools (Fullan, 1982; Leithwood, 1982; and Sarason, 1982). Holistic educators need to look at this literature because to effect change is a difficult and stressful task. Holistic education also requires its own approach to implementation.

The primary focus in implementing the holistic curriculum is on teacher personal growth. Of course, the curriculum is important as the second half of this book indicates, but a holistic curriculum in the hands of a transmission-oriented teacher will become a transmission curriculum.

Ideally, the principal or head teacher will be holistic. The principal should support teachers in their efforts to develop and use the holistic curriculum; if not, holistic teachers will function alone or in small isolated groups in schools. The principal can use teacher learning teams and help establish a co-operative environment among teachers in the school. The principal can do this by caring for the staff as the teacher cares for the student; in other words, the principal is fully present to the teachers. The principal asks the same questions of herself as she asks of the teachers. The principal takes risks and thus encourages risk-taking in teachers; she encourages risk-taking by being open and vulnerable. By being vulnerable, I don't mean the principal is weak, just that she is not afraid.

The holistic principal realizes that change is gradual and organic and thus approaches implementation from an ecological perspective. This means that interventions are made with an awareness of their possible effects. Narrow, mechanistic approaches to change are avoided because they do not recognize the interdependent nature of things. Thus, if the principal is establishing teacher learning teams, she gives thought to the possible effects to each team rather than hurriedly preparing the groupings. Strategies for professional growth are introduced which are not too threatening for staff. The principal intuitively senses what each teacher is prepared to do, what opportunities are appropriate for the staff's growth.

The principal has a vision of holistic education and attempts to live out this vision in her actions. If the principal is able to do this to any degree, it is a powerful facilitator for teacher growth. The deeper the integration between thought and action, the more powerful the effect on teachers. The vision should provide a sense of direction for the school and be open enough so that teachers can share in the vision and contribute to its development.

What might such a vision look like? I thought it would be appropriate to close this book by offering my own.

At this school we care about kids. We care about their academic work and we want them to see the unity of knowledge. In other words, we want to let students see how subjects relate to one another and to the students themselves. In relating subjects we find that the arts, or more generally the artistic sense, can facilitate these connections. We care about how kids think and, in particular, we try to encourage creative thinking. We want the students to be able to solve problems and use both analytical and intuitive thinking in the process.

We care about the physical development of the student and we devote part of the curriculum to activities that foster healthy bodies and a positive self-image. We hope to connect the students' body and mind so that they feel "at home" with themselves.

We care about how students relate to others and to the community at large. We focus on communication skills and, as the students develop, we encourage them to use these skills in a variety of community settings. At the same time we encourage the community to come into the school, particularly artists who can inspire the students' aesthetic sense.

Most of all, we care about the students' being. We realize that the final contribution that they make to this planet will be from the deepest part of their being and not from the skills we teach them. We can try to foster the spiritual growth of the student by working on ourselves as teachers to become more conscious and caring. By working on ourselves, we hope to foster in our students a deep sense of connectedness within themselves and to other beings on this planet.

References

Barrett, William. *Irrational Man: A Study in Existential Philosophy*. New York: Doubleday Anchor Books, 1962.

Emerson, R. W. *Selected Writing*. Edited by W. H. Gilman. New York: American Library, 1965.

Fullan, M. *The Meaning of Educational Change*. Toronto: OISE Press, 1982.

Heidegger, Martin. *Being and Time*. 12th unaltered ed. Tübingen: N. Niemeyer, 1972.

Kierkegaard, S. *Selection from Either/Or in Existential Encounters for Teachers.* Edited by Maxine Greene. New York: Random House, 1967.

Leithwood, K. A. "Implementing Curriculum Innovations." In *Studies in Curriculum for Decision-Making,* edited by K. A. Leithwood, pp. 245-67. Toronto: OISE Press, 1982.

Macrorie, K. *Twenty Teachers.* New York: Oxford University Press, 1984.

Noddings, Nel. *Caring: A Feminine Approach to Ethics and Moral Education.* Berkeley, Calif.: University of California, 1984.

Rogers, Carl. *On Becoming a Person.* Boston: Houghton Mifflin, 1961.

Rogers, Carl. *Freedom to Learn.* Columbus, Ohio: Charles Merrill, 1969.

Sarason, S. B. *The Culture of the School and the Problem of Danger.* 2nd ed. Boston: Allyn and Bacon, 1982.